THE OTHER SIDE OF EVERYTHING

The Other Side of Everything: Encouraging and Funny Stories to Help You Live Your Best Life

Copyright © 2025 Anne Mount

This book is set in the typeface *Athelas* designed by Veronika Burian and Jose Scaglione.

Paperback ISBN: 978-1-967262-18-2

A Publication of *Tall Pine Books*
PO Box 42 Warsaw | Indiana 46581
www.tallpinebooks.com

| 1 25 25 20 16 02 |

Published in the United States of America

THE OTHER SIDE OF EVERYTHING

ENCOURAGING AND FUNNY STORIES TO HELP
YOU LIVE YOUR BEST LIFE

ANNE MOUNT

"The best days were never scheduled; they just became stories..." —ANONYMOUS

"Anne's stories are so beautiful." —NANCIANN HORVATH, nurse, owner of *Improv For Health*

"Oh, do I relate!" —MICHAEL ARNOLD, Vietnam veteran, author, producer

"I love her reflections. So wonderful to read." —DEBBIE MCDERMOTT, retired elementary art school teacher

"Job well done!" —ED GRIFFIN, Air Force Vietnam veteran

"Thanks for bringing back memories...inspiring." —RUSS WHITFORD, world sailor

"I love Anne Mount's strength and courage regarding God working in her life." —BETH VENARD VINCENT, special education teacher

"Anne Mount is such a good writer! I love the part about her dad meeting Orville Wright!" —DAVE BOTT, retired engineer

"Her stories are so well written. What a blessing she writes for others." —SUSAN MARIE ASHENFELTER NOFZIGER, former missionary, works in marriage ministry

"Mount is making more of a difference than she knows." —RYAN HARBAUGH, retired Senior Account Executive, *UPS*

To Lindsay and Ashley, my dear sweet daughters who have been the joys of my life; to my awesome brothers, Dan and John, who have been my comfort and laughter through some hard days; to my amazing sons-in-law, Jeff and Shawn, who were smart enough and had the stamina enough (just kidding) to marry my daughters; and to my grandchildren, Brock and Logan, and Brynn and Sloane, God's most precious blessings, this book is for you.

May my stories live on in your hearts; and like ripples in a pond, may they give you hope and encouragement to make "your dreams" a reality. May you know that love can be found in our laughter as well as in our tears, and that no matter how far apart we may be or where our futures may take us, you will always be in my heart.

Love, your mom, sister, Anne, and Mimi (Meem)

O God, You have taught me from my youth;
And to this *day* I declare Your wondrous works.
Now also when I *am* old and gray-headed,
O God, do not forsake me,
Until I declare Your strength to *this* generation,
Your power to everyone *who* is to come. —PSALM 71:17-18

CONTENTS

LETTER TO MY READERS

As you embark on this journey in reading my book, I pray it will fill your hearts with enjoyable memories, and inspire more joyful journeys in your lives. It would be a huge favor to me, if you and future readers left a review on *Amazon*. While I have no expectations of what kind of review you leave, it would make my day knowing you read the whole book and shared your honest experience with the world. Thank you and God bless.

—Anne Mount

FOREWORD

Anne Mount came to my home in Southern California in 2013 to interview me about my book on my family and I liked her immediately. She was warm and understanding as I unfolded the story of my life growing up in the *Maybelline* family. She asked me questions as if we were close friends.

Since then, we have remained friends for many years, helping each other grow in our faith and friendship. Her book, *The Other Side of Everything*, is a masterpiece of detailed memories that we can all relate to. She has captured the "core" of what people feel in their dark moments – feelings so often impossible to put into words.

Her stories are a mirror to the soul. They touch on childhood memories, the struggles of growing up, the personal goals we chase as adults, and the dreams we continue to hold onto as we step into our later years. Her words are a balm for aching hearts needing to be understood, and appreciated.

They provide a pathway for all of us who are desperately

seeking to find our voices -- and have them be heard. Like Anne, I have leaned on my faith to prevail, believing I could grow through my struggles. Her stories remind us that God is always present, even in life's fiercest storms. And through faith and resilience, we not only heal ourselves but become a source of strength for others.

—SHARRIE WILLIAMS
Grandniece of Tom Lyle, creator of *Maybelline,*
Author of *The Maybelline Story and the Spirited
Family Dynasty Behind It* (*Bettie Youngs Books*)

INTRODUCTION
COUNTING OUR BLESSINGS

On a wintry evening in Ohio in 1956, my earliest memory as a child of three years of age, was seeing a stream of fire rolling across the road. My father, a physical therapist, would sometimes take me with him on his house calls to see his patients who were wheelchair users to help them exercise their muscles. Our trips were always fun. I loved any time I could spend with my dad. On this evening, however, around 5:00, a truck driver came speeding out of nowhere and ran the red light, hitting our red and white Ford station wagon! The impact caused our car to roll over on to its side. Gasoline started burning. Somehow, my father, a Marine, stuffed me into his big overcoat, kicked out the windshield, and got us out of the car! He carried me in his arms as he ran up a hill through woods in the cold frigid air toward a light in the window of a house. If there was some huge explosion, I do not remember it. We had escaped a near tragedy. That is all I knew.

A kind lady opened her home to us and offered me milk and cookies while my father used her telephone to call the police and my mom, I figured. I played dolls with her daughter who was about my age. A few days later, my mom and dad returned to the site of our car accident and found my badly scorched doll by the side of the road. I do not remember much about the lady on the hill, except that her home was filled with warmth and love. She was nice. In fact, kindness was everyone's "first instinct," in those days. Maybe that is why I do not remember being afraid.

As kids growing up in the 1950's and 1960's, yes, we had our troubles. I never expected mine to be narrowly escaping death. God obviously had plans for me. I just remember the days of friendly neighbors who would bring you a pie if you recently moved into the neighborhood, or invite you over to their home for fresh baked cornbread, or to go on a picnic, or to a barbecue. When color television sets were invented, I remember our neighbors across the street who just bought one. They invited us over to watch faces on the television screen turn pink or green. When I was six years old, my best friend was a black boy, David. For my brothers and me, our good friends were both white and black. We all played together and had loads of fun. We did not see color; we just saw our friends.

I remember summers before pesticides, when butterflies and praying mantises were in abundance. I remember catching fireflies on summer evenings and putting them in glass jars to light up our bedrooms with a soft glow.

I remember climbing trees, running through Groby's field, jumping into piles of autumn leaves, and sled riding down hills in winter. The sled riding was followed by hot cocoa our mom had waiting for us after taking off our coats and boots in a hallway called a "mud room." I remember when we placed our hands over our hearts and recited the *Pledge of Allegiance,* before classes began in school. Originally written by Captain George Thatcher Balch, a Union Army officer in the Civil War in 1885, to teach patriotism to children in school, it was later revised by Francis Bellamy in 1892 and goes like this: *I pledge allegiance to the Flag of the United States of America, and to the Republic for which it stands, one nation under God, indivisible, with liberty and justice for all.*

And, I remember when most everyone said, "Merry Christmas," "Happy Hanukkah," or "Happy Easter," and "Happy Passover," not just "Happy Holidays." I remember visiting a pet store, going to the local swimming pool, playing miniature golf, roller skating at the local roller-skating rink, and going to the local drive-in movie theater to see a movie with our parents, or our high school friends.

Those were the "good old days," as my two brothers, Dan and John, and I would build forts out of cardboard boxes, go hiking in the woods with our childhood friends without any fear, explore the local gravel pit, or gather all our friends and sit on the curb in the neighborhood while someone played folk songs on their guitar. And, who can forget the football games, high school plays, sock hops, homecomings, prom, and Neil Armstrong landing on the moon?

My book, *The Other Side of Everything*, is for anyone who wants to take a trip down memory lane and remember all the "good" in our lives and in our country, called, the United States of America. It is for anyone wanting to remember or desiring a simpler life through encouraging insights and funny stories of being children, teenagers, young professionals, spouses, parents, and finally grandparents and even great-grandparents.

Life is too short not to grab hold of it with your hopeful hands, my friends. Create memories with your loved ones, mend fences with family members, have fun with your neighbors and friends. Celebrate life, for it is the true treasure of our very being.

Finding Myself Again

By Anne Mount

Finding myself again,
Being older is not the end but
the beginning
coming around again,
Memories growing stronger
feed the dreams today and
bid me stay
a little while –
long enough to renew my smile.
And realize I never left the me that
was merely buried for so long
under the pretense of being strong,
when beneath fearful stories of trials
the years have shown, and kept me captive
by my fears.
Be gone all those tears.
As I write this poem I rise and learn

to fly...
No more will I allow one more year
of being young again slip by.
Because
no matter how old I appear,
I am younger than all my years.

PART I

THE GOOD OLD DAYS

1

CHICKENPOX, MEASLES, AND THE PRAYING MANTISES

My two brothers and I all got chickenpox at the same time. I was five-and-a-half years old. My brother, Dan, was not quite four years old, and my brother, John, was a toddler. It was an itchy time. John even had the annoying bumps in his ears. But our mother believed there was nothing a little *Calamine Lotion* could not fix.

I remember she nursed us back to health with chicken soup, too. Later, we all got the ten-day measles at the same time. It was not a thing we feared. Maybe it was not as bad then, as it can be today. To us, it was a little bit worse than the common cold. In fact, my mother wanted us all to get these annoyances over with at the same time, so they would never plague us again and our immune systems would be much stronger. We did and they were.

If we got colds or coughs, she made a poultice out of *Vicks VapoRub* that did the trick and helped us breathe easier at night and sleep. I do not remember panic and hysterics. I remember comfort and love.

The only hysterics I remember was when my praying mantis nests in six open glass jars on our dresser started to bloom earlier than expected one cold Spring morning. My older brother, Dan, and I slept in twin beds when we were very young. I shouted him awake with: "Look! It's snowing!" Hundreds of little white "baby" praying mantises had suddenly taken flight in our bedroom!

That sent our mother into a tailspin as she tried collecting them off the curtains and everyplace else. I took some of them to my kindergarten class for "show and tell." Now *that*, was something to get excited about!

2

HOW WE SPENT OUR SUMMER VACATIONS

M y mom was not just "camp director" in the summertime when we were kids. She was "Indiana Jones!" In those days the world was not a mine field full of wolves. It was more like a field full of daisies. She made us lunches in brown paper bags and sent us on our way to trek through the woods across the street.

Our group of explorers consisted of my two brothers, Dan and John, my friend, Mary, her older sister, Judy, and their brother, Bill. Their father owned acres of woods in my hometown of Dayton, Ohio, more specifically, Kettering, which was a suburb. Our town of Kettering was named after Charles F. Kettering, inventor of several innovations, most notably being the electric starter for the automobile. Deep in the woods we were free to swing on vines across the creek, and build forts out of moss, fallen logs, and sticks. We were also free to search out creatures like box turtles or garter snakes. We would look for arrowheads, unusual stones, and other assorted woodland things.

We never found the "Ark of the Covenant," nor did our mother. But she was smart. When we were safely on our various adventures, we became invisible to her and she got some much needed "me time." And, in our minds, we became "invincible!"

3

"JUST WAIT TIL YOU HAVE PETS OF YOUR OWN!"

As she daily scooped up dog hair into balls as big as tumbleweeds, my mother always said: "We have enough dog hair around here to make another dog!" My two brothers and I would snicker, look at our big hairy Golden Retriever, Taffy, and say: "Wow, Mom! That would be groovy!"

We obviously did not mind the hair, but it was annoying to our mom. We would just flick the dog hairs out of our drinks or off our food or pick them out of our pillows at night. I might have made a *Barbie* bed out of it. I think I once glued some dog hair on my *Ken* doll, who did not have any hair on his head. It was plastic. My brothers would make great *G.I. Joe* "pretend campfires" out of it.

If you were a kid, you could find at least fifty things to do with dog hair. But our mother could not stand it. When she got tired of scooping, she got out the vacuum cleaner. Instead of running for the hills, Taffy would just sit there. She loved her "vacuum massage." After a while she got so used to it that she would go sit by the closet door where our mom kept the vacuum cleaner and bark. It was time for her "vacuum massage." Our mom would just roll her eyes and say for the umpteenth time: "We have enough dog hair around here to make another dog!"

Her words must have sunk in the right way because years later, when my brothers and I each had families and homes of our own, we got dogs. My younger brother, John, was smart. He bought a small dog, a Yorkie, he named, Boo. But he discovered that Boo was not making enough hair, so he adopted a cat and named it, Tu. So, together, Boo and Tu made enough hair to make another dog. I bought a Labrador Retriever, thinking I was smart, getting a dog with short hair. But every time Sunny got excited, the hair on the back of his neck stood up and fell to the floor.

Just to torture myself even more, when Sunny turned ten years old, I bought another Labrador Retriever, a female I named, Laina, thinking Sunny would not be around much longer. But he got rejuvenated. At fourteen years old, he still got excited and well, you know what happened.

One day, I went to visit my brother, Dan, who rescued a dog, Shelby, a duplicate of our dog, Taffy. When Dan's son was a toddler, he made a great dust mop because his whole bottom would be covered in dog hair. My brother, looking a bit embarrassed, stood up. As he and Shelby made a beeline for the vacuum cleaner in the closet, I heard him say: "We have enough dog hair around here to make another dog!"

4

THOSE FOOLISH HAPPY DAYS

W hat else does one do with an empty refrigerator box when you are a kid and bored out of your mind in the summer of 1967? My brothers, Dan and John, twelve and ten at the time, decided that refrigerator box would be great if one brother got into it, and the other brother rolled it down the huge hill in our backyard.

So as Dan tells it, John was rolled up into the box like a hot dog, but instead of pushing him standing behind the box at the top of the hill, my brother tried to pull it "down" the hill! Well, the weight of the box with John in it picked up speed and rolled onto my brother Dan's finger, breaking it.

They were afraid to tell our dad because that meant a trip to the ER and lots of yelling from our dad. But it all worked out and my brothers laugh like crazy about this incident today.

Another time, my brothers were jumping on one of the twin beds in their bedroom, and Dan tossed John's pajamas into the ceiling light, a glass dish-shaped bowl thing covering a light bulb. The incandescent light bulb started to burn the cloth of the pajamas, but they managed, somehow, to get the pajamas out just in time. I'm sure the smell of smoke wafted through the air, and I think our mom said something like: "Go to bed!"

And, then there was the incident with someone's underwear being thrown up into our big industrial fan our father had installed in the hallway ceiling. Later, our Golden Retriever, Jessie, ended up wearing them.

And, I don't know if any of you gals remember, but as teenagers, us girls thought the way to get a tan in the summer was to combine baby oil with iodine in a bottle and spray it on our bodies. We "fried" ourselves in the name of "beauty." I did this to myself the day of my high school graduation. I was so sunburned I could barely walk up to the podium to receive my diploma. My poor boyfriend at the time had no clue how to dance with me at our school dance afterwards, when I told him: "Don't touch me!" Those were the days, when we were free and foolish, but surprisingly happy.

5

PHOTOS LEFT IN MY FATHER'S CAMERA

I got his *Kodak* camera in the brown leather case when he died, and the American flag that flew on our small fishing boat. It was the camera my father used when he and my mom attended the 1952 Rose Bowl Parade in Pasadena. It was the year they lived in Benicia, while my father attended physical therapy school. It was also the year they decided to move back to Ohio because many of our relatives still lived there. Then, little by little, the relatives all moved away, mostly to California and Washington.

Our house was small, white, with green shutters, on a corner lot across the street from the elementary school. Daisies filled the front yard by a white and red wooden sandbox with a roof that my father built. A modest vegetable garden grew along the side yard. We had our red and white Ford station wagon in the driveway. I had a square, green rubber swimming pool that my parents put in our front yard in the summertime guarded by our dog, Taffy, and some chickens.

I still remember my father driving his orange riding lawn mower. He attached my heavy-duty steel *Pull Wagon* so he could pull my cousins and me around the yard while he mowed the grass. Sometimes, people would gawk at us as they drove by on our street. I guess not many people had ever seen a riding lawn mower before, not in the early 1950's anyway.

The photos in my father's camera had been in their tiny metal canisters with the yellow tops for over fifty years, like some buried treasure. I wondered, when I got the film developed, would I be able to see anything? There were the yellowish colored photos of the Rose Bowl parade. There was a photo of my Italian father, so handsome with his black wavy hair in his college letter burgundy sweater with "UD" for University of Dayton in a pale blue, and wide leg brown trousers, standing with his college buddies. There was a beach, a park, and my beautiful blue-eyed mother, auburn hair, in a fitted pale blue suit standing next to some yellow Dahlias.

As I flip through the photos, I see the Ford station wagon, and next to our car is my mother holding me. I am two years old with hair as blonde as the sun. Then, I see a photo of me standing next to my grandmother, pretty and plump with her gray hair pulled back into a bun, wearing a white apron over a pink floral dress by our tall daisies. And, I see one more photo of me splashing in my green swimming pool, too young to know anything but pure joy.

Then, I see "the photo." My father is holding my hand. Our backs are turned, but I can see we are laughing. We are gazing at a pond reflecting the willow trees of summer, and I can see everything.

6

THE CHAIR

It is Christmastime, 1955. My father looks so young, wearing his neat 1950's white shirt and brown trousers. He sits on our gray sofa by the Christmas tree, reading his newspaper. My mother's "Grandma Moses" drapes that she made herself, hang in the background. Next to my father is me, two years old, blonde curls, sitting in "my chair," pale blue pajamas, pretending to read my picture book. My chair is the perfect size, even though my feet dangle over the edge. The chair is a pale rose color, with sturdy, short dark wooden legs, and brass buttons along the arms. My dad and I smile at my mother, who is taking this picture.

My father passed away in February 2006 from Alzheimer's disease. He could not do much toward the end, but he could smile with his eyes. The last time I saw him he smiled and winked at me. I kissed his forehead. We looked at each other for a long time. We both just knew.

In thinking of my father, I always think of my chair. That chair has traveled from Dayton, Ohio; to Cleveland; to New

York City, San Francisco, Dallas, and finally it came to rest in my garage in my home near Los Angeles. It was in my garage for a while, the stuffing coming out of one arm. It had been covered with a blanket, and sadly, pushed aside. In the process of unpacking, I found the photo of my father and me, us sitting in the living room when I was small, him on the gray sofa, me in my rose-colored chair. And, I thought to finally get my chair reupholstered. I went to see Rose, an Italian lady, at her shop, and picked out the perfect fabric, a salmon color and dotted Swiss pattern, to go with the bedspread in my guest room that doubles as my office.

The other day, my chair, newly upholstered, with new brass buttons and refurbished legs, arrived. Tonight, on the anniversary of my father's passing, I finally put my chair in my office. After years of thinking of it as "just a chair," and not sitting in it, I finally sat in it again. I felt the brass buttons on the arms. I felt the comfortable seat, and remembered my father.

7

WHEN TRIPS MAKE MEMORIES

As I get older, I find myself thinking more often about the vacations I went on with my parents and two brothers, Dan and John, when we were young. Every summer, we took a two-week vacation, mostly with an old green canvas tent that weighed a ton. It often reminded me of setting up for some circus with tent poles, and stakes you had to pound into the ground. We had a station wagon, that also fit sleeping bags, a *Coleman* stove, a *Coleman* water jug, a picnic basket with tablecloth, utensils, plates, a portable potty and suitcases. I think my dad must have tied the tent to the top of our car. The name, "Griswold," comes to mind.

Many trips consisted of fishing or water skiing on Lake Cumberland in Kentucky. But other adventures included going to the Adirondack Mountains; Niagara Falls; Mt. Rushmore National Memorial in the Black Hills of South Dakota; Cheyenne, Wyoming, and the whole state of Florida along the coast in summer!

My mother, brothers and I helped my father set up the

tent, sometimes in rainstorms; at night by our car headlights, and once, by accident, near some train tracks at the top of a hill we didn't see. When that train whistle blew at dawn from the train barreling down the tracks, we all jumped up like a bunch of jackrabbits!

I remember my brothers chased lizards beneath mossy trees in Florida, while I lounged at the beach with my *Seventeen* magazines. I remember listening to a lecture by a park ranger at Mt. Rushmore under the stars, and being amazed how Daniel Boone (Fess Parker), my brother John's hero, rode his horse over to my brother and spoke to him during the "Cheyenne Frontier Days" rodeo. My brother, John, ten years old at the time, was wearing his fake fur Coonskin hat, just like Fess. Well, Fess sees my brother, rides right over to him, smiles and says:

"Did ya kill it yourself?" We all laughed and my brother got a memory to last a lifetime. I think to this day he might still have that Coonskin hat!

My parents gave us a love for nature as we hiked on trails, fished in lakes, swam in lakes, collected seashells on a beach, and experienced the magnificence of mountains. And a breakfast of eggs and bacon never tasted so good as when eaten in the quiet surroundings of a forest.

I am grateful I listened to the quiet in the mountains and deep in the woods. Those are the trips memories are made of, that can truly make us feel alive. It is the essence of what Henry David Thoreau expressed when he wrote: *I went to the woods because I wished to live deliberately, to front only the essential facts of life, and see if I could not learn what it had to teach, and not, when I came to die, discover that I had not lived.*

8

DAYTON, OHIO, MY HOMETOWN OF ECCENTRICS

My hometown is Dayton, Ohio. It is the home of such eccentric notables as Orville and Wilber Wright, inventors of the airplane; Charles F. Kettering, inventor of the electric starter for cars, Freon refrigerant for refrigerators and air conditioning; and John H. Patterson, founder of NCR – National Cash Register Company, who practically employed the whole town.

According to Mark Bernstein's book, *Grand Eccentrics, Turning the Century: Dayton and the Inventing of America (Orange Frazer Press, 2003)*, Orville and Wilber flew kites as adults, dressed in suits each day like they were going to a wedding; and at Kitty Hawk, Orville numbered the eggs their chickens laid so they could be eaten in the order they were produced.

Charles F. Kettering, a great American industrialist, often assigned research tasks to his people who had no background in the problems they needed to work on.

When a man named, Thomas Midgley, complained that

he knew nothing about fuel chemistry, Kettering replied: "That's okay, neither does anyone else!"

As crazy as they seemed, they were what Patterson called, "upstreamers," ones who go against the currents. If they didn't have the answers, they figured them out. When asked what they lived for, Patterson said: "To do good." And, good they did. When the Dayton flood hit in 1913, Patterson built over 300 flat bottom boats and organized rescue teams to save people stranded on rooftops. He fed and housed hundreds of people who were left homeless.

When I was a teenager, in the 1970's, Kettering's descendants built a beautiful hospital. I had the opportunity to meet Virginia Kettering, the wife of Charles F. Kettering's son, Eugene, when she gave tours of the hospital when they first opened. And, when my father was young, working his way through college, he delivered a package one day to a particular home. Who should open the door but Orville Wright!

9

WE HAD CLASSIC CARS AND
CLASSIC LIVES

Once a year we have a classic car show in my little
town in California that reminds me of that fictional
town on the television sitcom we used to watch in the 1960's,
The Andy Griffith Show. Gawking at all the shiny cars and
beautiful makes, models and colors always brings back
many wonderful memories. The 1950's, especially, was a
decade that brought renewed hope to America.

Husbands started cooking with bravado on their new
barbecue grills at family and neighborhood gatherings.
People were kind, for the most part, and happy. They felt
enthusiastic, and the classic cars of the 1950's showed it.

Cars were built like tanks, then. They were colorful, cool,
dynamic with a touch of pizzazz! When I was a little kid, my
parents bought their first classic car. It was a 1957 turquoise
and white Chevrolet Bel Air. I have seen home movies of my
brother, Dan, who was three years old, and me, five years
old, washing the family car with our father. I think we got

more suds on us from the bucket of water and sponges than on the car!

Later, my parents bought the "big green bomb," a Dodge Club Coupe. It had such soft fabric on the seats that my brothers and I often fell asleep on the way home from swimming all day at our community swimming pool in the summertime. I just remember feeling safe and comforted in that warm soft fabric.

Looking back, as a middle class family living in the Midwest in America, we felt blessed. Life was simple. Neighbors helped neighbors. There was a sense of an open friendly community where if you needed help someone was always there.

For one moment in history, our country was one where the endless possibilities of freedom made one believe in the American dream.

10

COFFEE MAKES THE WORLD GO 'ROUND

W hen I was growing up, my parents drank *Folgers*, or *Maxwell House*. The sound of my mom's percolator was as familiar as the toast popping up in the toaster. The aroma of coffee, though I was too young to drink any, filled our kitchen with a warmth that became part of our family tradition. It is one tradition or ritual that has been in my home, and is now in my grown children's homes, with my little granddaughter enjoying her cup of steamed milk from her daddy's expresso machine.

Just for fun, I was watching coffee commercials through the ages on *YouTube* the other day. Some of you might remember the taglines: "*Maxwell House*, good to the last drop!" "Tastes as good as it smells." Years ago, they even showed you how to make the coffee in the commercial, and the directions were usually on the can or jar. In fact, the metal cans became very useful containers for my mom's cooking grease or my dad's nails and screws on his workbench. Nothing was wasted.

In an old *Folgers* commercial, some poor wife was beside herself because she could not make her husband a decent cup of coffee. Unfortunately, coffee making was a woman's job back in the day. Well, who should come along to the rescue but dear old Mrs. Olsen, who saved the day and taught the poor wife how to make "good rich mountain grown coffee." Later, men could do just as well, as we learned in the 1987 movie, *Moonstruck*, when Cher, in her role as Loretta, says to her boyfriend, Johnny, played by Nicolas Cage: "You're a slob, but you make good coffee!"

As time marched on, people were in a hurry, so "instant coffee" was touted to taste just as good. The slogan of *Folgers* was: "Tastes as good as fresh perked!" Then, *Sanka* was the new kid on the block, a "two-fisted cup of coffee," for the men. They promoted this brand as one that you could drink up to ten cups a day and still be steady as a rock. But later, the actor, Robert Young, of the television show, *Father Knows Best*, encouraged everyone to be healthier and drink decaffeinated coffee so as not to mess up your nerves.

I don't know how many cups of coffee my mom and her friends drank in the mornings when my brothers and I were at school, but I'm sure it was enough to discuss the dramatic tales of the TV soap opera, *As The World Turns*, in her "coffee klatch" group. It was probably also enough for her to stay energized to help us with our homework after school.

I drank my first cup of coffee as a freshman in college so I could pull an "all-nighter" for an exam I had to study for. I had to put lots of milk in it. I figured coffee was an acquired taste. It was while I was living in New York City as a writer and editor that I learned there were shops that specialized in particular coffee brands and teas. You could pick and choose what coffee beans you wanted. I was like a kid in a candy store. It was amazing! And, coffee makers became all the rage. I think I got four or five of them when I got married. They were called, *Mr. Coffee.*

As a young mom, I was so thankful for coffee. It certainly was my "go-to" drink. Over the years, coffee has been the focal point of many family gatherings in the warmth of my mother's kitchen and in mine, and in my children's kitchens today. I think it's true what the poet T.S. Eliot once wrote: *I have measured out my life with coffee spoons.*

11

A SUMMER OF HORSES

One vivid memory I have of my childhood in the summer was driving down a country road at sunset in our turquoise and white Chevy. The heat and humidity had been unbearable during the day. We did not have air conditioning in our home. We had a huge industrial ceiling fan my dad installed in the hallway. I guess we were tough, as we sweated our way through the summer accepting it as the way things were. My dad was away on a fishing trip, so my mom put my two brothers and me into the car and rolled down all the windows. We felt the cool evening breezes as they blew against our faces and tossed our hair as we sped out into the countryside.

I was thinking how wonderful it would be to spend my summer vacation as a child again, when my oldest daughter, Lindsay, approached me with a question. She was twelve years old at the time, in July 1995, in our home in the suburbs of Dallas, Texas. "Mom, may I *please* take horseback riding lessons from Lauren's mom at the barn?" she begged. Her friend's mom bought an Arabian and had been going to their barn frequently and inviting my daughter to come along.

Lindsay had been talking nonstop about a Palomino, Big Boy. She was drawing pictures of horses and even drew up a business proposal on poster board to convince her father and me how she would contribute to her cause with her allowance. Her sister, Ashley, nine years old at the time, had also expressed interest in taking horseback riding lessons.

After dinner one summer evening, Lindsay, Ashley, their father, and I drove out to the country. I watched my daughters' faces grow more excited as we approached the barn. And, my own memories of grooming horses, feeding them, riding them, came flooding back to me. An early morning sunrise scene comes to mind, as my riding instructor made me clean my horse's hooves, and learn how to put the saddle and bridle on before I could ride. But it was always worth it. "I get dibs on Ryder," my nine-year-old friend, Mary, would say. "I get dibs on Pretty Boy!" I would call back.

As we approached the barn, I saw several horses grazing peacefully in the field, people riding horses, two dogs running around, a pot belly pig rooting by the fence, a lady grooming her horse in a stall. It was an active place. We all got out of the car and walked over to the paddock, where Lindsay's friend, Lauren, stood by the fence, watching her parents ride their horses.

Just watching them, being in the country, brought an immediate sense of peace. Lindsay, Lauren, and Ashley went to get Big Boy in the pasture and bring him over so we could meet him. As I watched their three silhouettes in the field against a soft purple and orange sky, I remembered again how precious is the gift of time in the innocence of life. How precious are each of our lives if we take the time to be grateful.

12

WHY I LIVE IN A SMALL TOWN

In our quiet town of Kettering, my two brothers, Dan and John and I played in the woods across the street from our home. We built forts in Groby's Field when it was an apple orchard, and went on adventure treks to People's drugstore for ice cream in the summer. We saw the movie, *101 Dalmatians*, in 1961, at the Victoria Theatre in Dayton, and went to horse shows at the Montgomery County Fairgrounds. At the end of summer, we would make ourselves almost sick from riding the *Rock-o-Plane* at the annual county fair. And right before we had to go back to school, our mom took us clothes shopping at Rike's department store. I still remember my favorite purchase, a flowery blue blouse, blue pleated skirt, and brown penny loafers.

When I was sixteen years old, I began publishing my poems in *The Cincinnati Enquirer*. At the time, humorist, Erma Bombeck, was writing for the *Kettering-Oakwood Times*. I decided to write her a letter seeking her advice. Imagine my delight when she answered me in a letter back! Erma wrote: *You are on your way at sixteen. I could not write my name on my gym suit! Good luck and God bless. Erma Bombeck.* Spurred on by Erma's encouraging words, I longed to leave Kettering and set out, after college, for New York City.

Living in the Big Apple from 1977 to 1982, was a blast. As a senior associate editor at *Lady's Circle*, my three staff members and I covered such press events as Phil Donahue's book talk at Tavern on the Green; a promotion of General Electric's new light bulb at Radio City Music Hall, which included a gigantic hot air balloon; and the opening of the famous, Studio 54. My then husband, David, was wearing a very nice tie I bought him for his birthday at the Studio 54 opening, and Grace Jones came right up to him and with scissors in hand, cut it in half! She was known for crazy stunts like that, I guess.

When I was working at *Harper's Bazaar* as an assistant features editor, I often saw rock star Mick Jagger's ex-wife, Jerry Hall, as she strutted past my office to our fashion department to visit editors. And yes, at times, it was just like in the movie, *The Devil Wears Prada,* as we were all afraid of our managing editor who was known to take nips from a flask in her desk.

Before having kids, we lived through the big "Blackout" of July 1977. We also experienced the subway strike. My publisher, Mr. Lopez, at *Lady's Circle*, paid for taxi cabs for us, but just for fun I once walked all the way from our apartment on the upper East Side on 81st street, to 28th and Broadway, where our offices were located in a little Brownstone. We were also living in the city during the time John Lennon got shot. There is a memorial to him in Central Park.

The fun part of living in New York City was that we enjoyed many Broadway shows via *Half-Price Tickets* and saw the famous Rockettes perform. We had dinners in many amazing restaurants like the Rainbow Room on the 65th floor at Rockefeller Center, and the famous Grand Central Oyster Bar, Inc. And viewing Manhattan from Top of the World Trade Center Observatories was an extraordinary once-in-a-lifetime experience that is forever gone.

When David and I moved with our two young daughters in July 1986, from our first home in Mt. Kisco, New York, to the San Francisco Bay Area, to San Rafael, we rumbled with the 1989 Loma Prieta earthquake, met Robin Williams at Taco Bell, and enjoyed ferry boat rides to Pier 39 where my kids loved riding on the carousel. My daughter, Lindsay, went to kindergarten with Carlos Santana's son, Salvador. On career day, Carlos played his guitar for the kids in their classroom, another unforgettable experience. Us moms always enjoyed talking with him when he picked his kids up from our elementary school. Carlos was always so nice.

After several years, we moved to Plano, Texas, in December 1994, donned cowboy boots, went to a rodeo and started to say, "y'all" a lot. The highlight of my time there was having Zig Ziglar as my Sunday school encouragers class teacher at my church. He would say things like: "Make today worth remembering."

Years later, after my daughters were all grown up and on their own, I landed in a small, Mayberry-like town in California, where the people are friendly and helpful. The houses have white picket fences, quaint shops, and Christmas decorations that make our town look like a *Hallmark* movie in winter.

I love my current town, and realize why I finally landed here. It reminds me of Kettering, when I was a child. And, while we do not have a People's drugstore, we do have a little country grocery store where the owners know my name, and I know theirs.

13

OUR KITCHEN HELD OUR MEMORIES

My father was Italian. His favorite word was, "mangia," which means, "eat!" It was the only Italian word I ever learned. We had no trouble eating my mom's lasagna, as she made the best! And, she loved to make spaghetti and meatballs, my father's second favorite dish. My mom lived in the house we grew up in for over fifty-five years, so I have memories of much love and laughter, and some tears. So much living happened in our kitchen, and in the kitchens of my relatives, mostly the Italian side.

I remember as a small child looking up at my Aunt Lucia, rolling out the dough on a big table to make her raviolis. I remember other relatives gathered around a big pot of tomato sauce in my mother's kitchen, discussing the cares of the day as they each took turns stirring the sauce with a big wooden spoon.

Our kitchen was an active, sometimes hazardous place. When I was in sixth grade, my mom was helping me with my math homework on our kitchen table. A pot of oil on the stove caught fire as my mom was heating the oil to make French Fries. I applied what I had just learned from a fire fighter who gave a talk to my class, which was to "smother" the grease fire. I quickly grabbed our green area shag rug and threw it on the pot, putting the fire out.

Our kitchen also became our church in a way, as we prayed to God to save my brother, Dan. He went to the hospital to have what the doctor said, "was a simple tonsillectomy." The doctor led us all to believe that my brother would be happily eating ice cream in no time. But something went wrong.

My brother was not waking up because the anesthesiologist gave him too many drugs to put him to sleep for the surgery. While my dad stayed with my brother at the hospital, my mom, her best friend, Joanne, and I stayed up most of the night praying for my brother to wake up. He eventually did, twenty-four hours later, and had no residual problems. He grew up to become a successful architect. I thank God for hearing our urgent prayers in the kitchen that night.

In May of 1981, my mom had a brain aneurysm. A neurosurgeon saved her life, but I do believe it was God. Her condition was still "touch-and-go," when she was in the hospital. About this time, I remember having to tell my father that his youngest brother, Eugene, passed away after receiving a telephone call in our kitchen. It was heartbreaking, as we were already worried about my mom.

I had to tell this news to my father. He put his head in his hands and cried. We were sad to lose my uncle, but God did spare my mother who had a full recovery. It was a miracle.

Over the years, I brought my children to my parents' home, as did my brothers with their children. We had many years of laughter, and dancing in my mom's kitchen. We celebrated birthdays, and holidays, and my father's life, when he passed away from Alzheimer's disease on February 25, 2006.

When my mom turned ninety-two, on March 20th, 2016, I made a trip home to celebrate her birthday with her. She opened the front door with a big smile on her face and enthusiastically announced: "I made you a pot roast!" We celebrated her life, our life together, at our table in the kitchen.

Every time I came home to visit my mom. I prayed to God to let me have a little bit more time with her. Though I did not want to listen, I believe God was trying to tell me that "this" one visit would be the last one. On April 27, 2016, my mom changed her address and went to Heaven to be with her loving God and my father.

I thought about all the meals she had made for me; all the cakes and cookies she baked with hands full of love; all the times she was there when my brothers and I came home from school, and when she welcomed my family home for the holidays. Standing alone in our kitchen for the last time, I tearfully thanked her. All the memories came flooding back to me, from playing around the house on a dirt pile when it was in the frame stage, to the day we moved in, to the comings and goings of our lives, like some fast-forward movie speeding all the way up to the present, then the memories abruptly stopped. I gazed around our kitchen in the silence one last time, then slowly walked out the front door.

14

PLACES IN THE HEART

I was thinking the other day about some of my favorite movies that take place in the summer, like *Field of Dreams, American Graffiti, Gidget, A Summer Place*. Yes, I am dating myself, but these are the movies from my youth. Even the movie, *On Golden Pond*, though it is about a married couple in their golden years, reminds me of a summer vacation I spent as a teenager.

Our family stayed at a cottage on Lake Gage in Indiana. In my heart I am remembering a "summer crush" who had a red Fiat, blonde hair, and blue eyes. I remember walks around the lake with my mother, sailboats catching the wind in their sails, and the afternoons my mom taught me how to crochet a purse. We sat in wicker chairs on the screened-in porch, while my dad and brothers went fishing. The purse was yellow, and I felt so proud of myself when I finished it.

I remember my mother giving us summer passes for the community swimming pool where my brothers, our friends and I would hang out all day swimming, sunbathing, grabbing snacks at the snack bar. She would pick us up at dinnertime and sometimes take us to get hamburgers at a place called, Sandy's. The burgers cost fifteen cents, and they never tasted so good after a fun "day-in-the-sun."

I remember playing miniature golf next to the drive-in movie theatre and getting my first "hole in one," before my friends and I would jump back into the car to watch the movie. Sometimes, we would sit on the hood of the car to watch the movie, under the stars.

On Fourth of July my brothers and I would catch fireflies, eat watermelon, and watch the fireworks explode across the summer sky. One of my earliest summertime memories when I was five years old is of my mother's vegetable garden. She grew tomatoes and green beans. We used to sit on the porch and snap the beans for dinner, as my brothers laid in the grass and pointed out shapes in the clouds. She also grew beautiful tulips, pinks, and yellows, mostly.

There was a lightness to summer in those days. The air was cleaner. The sun seemed to shine brighter. The days were peaceful. And, we saw more butterflies and birds. I remember birds filled the skies with flight and song!

There was a lightness in our lives, that no one could take away from us. It was a time when a loving heart felt, before the mind could think. We call it, "the good old days."

PART II

MY FAMILY IN A NUTSHELL

15

LETTERS FROM THE TOOTH FAIRY, CALIFORNIA

(1994)

"That was your handwriting on the letter from the tooth fairy, wasn't it, Mom?" my nine-year-old daughter, Ashley, asked me, so many years ago. "Is the tooth fairy *real*?" she persisted. My heart sank, as I began to realize that I had gone as far as I could go in keeping the magic alive for my children. I tried to fudge it for a few more minutes, but I could tell she did not believe me.

For years, I had been writing letters to my children from the tooth fairy, which they liked better than the dollar or two I put into an envelope under their pillows. They even wrote letters back to the tooth fairy. For example: *Dear Tooth Fairy, please do not take my tooth. I want to save it to show my kids when I'm grown up. But, please leave your letter to me and some money so I can buy more yarn to make a friendship bracelet. Your biggest fan. Love, Ashley*

Once, the tooth fairy forgot to leave a letter and money. My daughter was so disappointed and I felt terrible. The next night, I wrote this letter, with a couple of dollars, and slipped it under her pillow: *Dear Ashley, No, I did not forget you. I was at a meeting with all the other tooth fairies, a convention. We fairies all get together once a year in a very special place. Even fairies need a vacation. But, I'm so proud of you. You lost another tooth! Congratulations! And, I understand that you got good grades recently. Keep up the good work, kiddo! And make everyday a good day. You are special. Love, your tooth fairy.*

My daughter was so thrilled that there were lots of tooth fairies, I overheard her tell her dad: "And, guess what, Dad? They even go to a special place for vacation!" Over the years, the tooth fairy brought great comfort to both my daughters. As they gained more self-confidence, however, they were ready to move on and gave her up. I, on the other hand, was not ready to give her up, but I was trying. She always gave me a lot of comfort, too, because every day a mother must be brave.

16

BUILDING A HOUSE CAN NEARLY
RAZE A FAMILY, TEXAS

(1995)

During the time we were putting the finishing touches on our newly built home in Plano, Texas, I was initially accused of watering my plant too much when I complained to the construction foreman about a leak in our dining room ceiling. It was a "fake plant." I was told that my eyes were failing me when I asked our contractors about the fading wallpaper in the master bathroom. It faded. And, it was suggested by Dr. Plumber that my children must have the flu when they were experiencing dizziness and headaches, when I wondered about a possible gas leak above the ceiling of my oldest daughter, Lindsay's bedroom. There was a leak.

As it turned out, the leak in the roof in our dining room was so bad, that water had dripped down the inside of my dining room wall, and the rotten wood had to be replaced. The wallpaper had faded so badly in the bathroom that it was a dead ringer for the blank side of the wallpaper. And, when the gas man took his little meter reader up to the attic above my daughter's bedroom, the needle sprang to attention, justifying my delusions.

He shut off the gas, and would not turn it back on until the pipe in the furnace could be tightened and better insulated. This, "it's-all-in-your-head" mentality toward women actually existed, and was a major complaint of other moms in the neighborhood going through the "new house blues." Just building a home in any family's lifetime can take its toll on the members. My then husband, David, for example, did not believe me at first, about the gas leak. "This is a new house!" he shot back. "How could there be anything wrong?" How could there be anything "right," I thought, until all the "bugs," go away.

In our wildest dreams we never expected to almost lose our two dogs as they ran out the back door in the great dishwasher flood or feel the thrill of our very own giant "kazoo," every time the wind screamed through our front door. We also did not expect to be "extras" in our own home movie like, *The Money Pit*, when construction workers showed up out of the blue and sledge hammered our dining room wall as we were having breakfast.

When my neighbor's chandelier fell and crashed to the floor in their foyer, missing their two daughters by seconds, I tried to calm my friend. "I know it seems like it is real, Betsy, but just remember, it is not. It is just virtual reality!

Truth is, there were some screws loose and not just on the chandelier. Of course, no one would tell us anything. How could they when we just imagined it? As I was trying to imagine all the kinks worked out by the time our kids went off to college, my then husband in a pensive mood, said: "All-in-all, even though we've had our troubles with the house I really like it." I wanted to throw a few hallucinations at him, but kept my calm. I simply replied: "Yes, dear, it's the vision that counts!"

17

THE ONE THING THAT IS ALWAYS LOST IN MY HOUSE IS...

I n the 1990's, we called it the *"remote control."* It was a hand-held television control device that was about the size of a candy bar.

I call it the *huge-a-diggy*. Some people call it the *watcha-ma-call-it*. Other people, when they get desperate, call it *the thing*. "You know what I *mean!*" my then husband used to say, getting impatient. "Oh, you mean the "remote control!" I retort, my memory finally coming back to me. "It's either doing double duty as a door stop or a bump under the sofa cushion, or just became the "fill-in" channel changer for our daughter, Lindsay's remote control that needs a new battery.

Whatever you call it, the irritating little gadget is never around when you want it. One day, our dog thought it was a bone and tried to bury it under some blankets on a chair. Another day, the darn thing ended up trying to disguise itself in a bowl of popcorn. Someday, I just *know* it will end up in somebody's pocket banging around in the dryer, if the washing machine doesn't get it first. I can just hear the TV repair man now: "So, you say it went through the rinse cycle twice? Ma'am, I don't think these things are waterproof!"

My remote control in our bedroom looked like a chocolate bar with buttons. The one in the family room for the BIG TV looked like a remote control for Arnold Schwarzenegger. If you accidently stepped on it, you might end up, "terminated!" In fact, I saw a crazy cartoon once, where two kids got a hold of the remote control, a real zinger! When the boy pushed the button, the girl turned into a monkey and began chasing him. When she snatched the remote control from her brother, she pushed a button and he turned into a bear and tried to eat the kitchen table.

These kids kept grabbing the remote control, pushing the buttons, and changing themselves into different creatures. They kept chasing each other throughout the house, as their mother, oblivious to the whole thing, kept ordering them to brush their teeth and get ready for school!

The kids raced upstairs. When they zapped each other at the same time the boy turned into a turtle and the girl turned into a snail. The remote control then flipped up into the air and fell to the floor in the center of the bedroom, just as the mother said she was coming upstairs to check on them.

Slowly, slowly, ever so slowly, they crawled toward the remote control to change themselves back into their original human forms before their angry mother barged through the bedroom door. Then, *click*! Sorry, I can't tell you the rest of the story until I find the *thing*!

18

THIS CAR ISN'T GOING TO LAST
MUCH LONGER

(1994)

W e have a car that is on its last legs, arms, feet, and hands. It is so far gone that it is spitting up oil every day. The doors creak when you open them, and part of the cover of the steering wheel comes off in your lap if you try to honk the horn. We would have dumped the car years ago, but we were putting money into other things, like making ends meet. Someday, I hope to donate the car to someone more desperate than us, but right now, it is more of a necessity than a liability.

We just keep getting things that break on it repaired, and try to maintain it as best we can, because it is still cheaper than getting a new car. Who knows? Maybe when we are lucky enough to afford a new car, we will just keep the old one around for posterity. We will all sit in the garage as a family, circle around the old car like a campfire, and tell stories to the kids.

"See this car?" I'd tell my oldest daughter. "This was the car your dad and I raced to the hospital in when I was in labor with you! Your father ate steak in between my contractions on a hot summer day in July, then we zipped off to the hospital at sunset. It was so quiet that evening at the hospital that it gave us time to think of a name for you as we walked the halls for seventeen hours. And, oh yeah, you were named after *The Bionic Woman*, because that was my favorite TV show in the 1970's."

"See this car?" I'd tell my youngest daughter. "Over the years we've probably eaten 800 tons of McDonald's hamburgers, 600 tons of French Fries, and drank one thousand sodas sitting on these very seats!" "See this car?" I'd tell my husband. "This was the car I used to drive around for hours in so our daughters would fall asleep in their car seats and I could get two minutes to myself!"

This was the car that took us out of New York City to the suburbs of Mt. Kisco, to airports at the start of wonderful family vacations and home to see my parents in Ohio. It was the car that took us to the circus, to plays, to soccer games, to PTA meetings. This is the car I cried in, when I dropped each of you, my precious daughters, off at nursery school for the first day; and when I drove to doctors' appointments for checkups and prayed that I'd get a clean bill of health to see you both graduate from college.

This was the car I picked you up in after school. This was the car that probably made 5,000 trips to the grocery store, 2,000 trips to the beauty salon, 25,000 trips to the mall! When all is said and done, it's been a good old car. We probably should find a green pasture for it, so it can live out its days in peace, instead of trying to keep up with the other cars on the highway at rush hour.

Every single night, my daughters and I put our hands on

the bumper and pray: "Please, God, just let this car last one more day!" My then husband pipes up and says: "You *know*, this car isn't going to last much longer!"

19

A FATHER'S DAY SALUTE, CALIFORNIA

(1991)

I was having a bad day at Bubba's, a family eatery in our quaint town called, San Anselmo. It was 90 degrees. My two daughters, Ashley, age five, and Lindsay, age seven-and-a-half, were going crazy with their crayons and root beer floats when who should sit down at the booth next to us but calm, collected Steve, father of triplets. His kids, three years old, were quiet, well-behaved, did not eat their crayons and waited patiently for their food to arrive. His wife was not there. He did not seem to need her. At all. We spoke briefly, then went back to our kids as I imagined my kids with paper bags over their heads.

I waited for Steve to go crazy when his son spilled a glass of juice, but he remained calm. That must be his secret, I thought. He never gets ruffled. He never gets *PMS* either. In my mind I gave Steve a gold medal in the restaurant venue.

Another day, I was doing my "frazzled-mom-in-the-Volvo" routine, afraid I would be late picking up my kids at school. As I screeched into a parking spot, who should be standing calmly on the sidewalk chatting with all the moms but Carlos Santana. We moms never got used to him picking up his kids at school. He was the highlight of our day. He was always so "down-to-earth," so nice. Carlos could sense I was a bit "unstrung," and tried to cheer me up. He did. I gave Carlos the gold medal in the frantic, after school venue.

Still another day, I was racing home from running errands with my kids and totally forgot about dinner. My poor kids were starving and I was feeling like "Mother Dreke." I pulled into a fast-food taco joint. As we stumbled to the counter so I could place an order, I ran into "Mrs. Doubt-fire," calmly waiting for a huge order of tacos. Oh boy, I thought, I finally run into Robin Williams and my hair looks like it went through a meat grinder! "Hi," I said meekly. His face lit up with a smile that made me want to melt into my sneakers! What a nice dad, I thought, picking up food for his wife and kids. I gave Robin a gold medal in the fast-food venue.

And, one evening, I was driving home, my brain fried from watching three hours of my daughters going through their jazz dance routines. My then husband, David, was working late, and I was beyond clueless when we walked through the door as to what I was going to fix for dinner. Suddenly, I smelled the most wonderful smell of mashed potatoes and baked chicken. "Hi," my then husband said. "Welcome home." I was dumbstruck.

"I thought you had to work late," I stammered. "That's tomorrow night," he corrected. "Bless you," I said, as we all sat down at the dinner table. I gave my then husband, David, a gold medal for the home cooked meal venue.

20

HELP! I'M TRAPPED IN THE AFTER SCHOOL CARPOOL LANE!
(TEXAS, 1996)

I can fly to New York City and back, attend a Rangers game, or go shopping at the mall by the time I move an inch in the carpool lane when I pick up my older daughter, Lindsay, almost thirteen, at school. The snail's pace, over-crowded mess of this situation is not just an occasional event. It happens every day. It's a real nail biting, muscle tensing kind of happening, as anxious moms worm their way in and out of tiny spaces between cars so they can work their way over to the curb, so their little darlings won't get crushed when they try to cross the carpool path.

It is every mom for herself in this hair-raising display of motherly devotion, which reminds me of a bunch of ants who just had their shelter rock removed and are scurrying like mad to get their precious eggs under the ground. As for me, I always zoom into the far left lane, which seems to crawl a little better, and get myself positioned opposite the school tree. Then, I am poised to zip over to the curb as soon as a mom picks up her cargo and moves out.

While all this craziness is going on I am looking for my daughter in the crowd of kids where everyone looks like a *Gadzooks* fashion ad, and good luck if you see a shred of individuality there. I try to look for her hair twisted in a bun with the ends sticking out. I try to look for her jeans, but every girl is into retro sixties bell bottoms, covered down to the knees in one of their dads' old shirts.

As I am sitting in my car, feeling like a baked potato, I get a telephone call on my cell phone from my younger daughter, Ashley, age ten, who is already home, having taken the bus home from her school. "Hi, sweetie!" I say. "It's so nice to hear your voice; I'll be home soon!" "Mom, where are the popsicles you got? I can't find them!" she rants. But, before I can answer, she adds: "And Sunny has diarrhea again. He just exploded all over the laundry room floor!" "That's nice, dear," I say, distracted. "I'll be home soon." I close my cell phone.

I blast out over to the curb, beating out another mom who honks her horn and gives me a dirty look. I finally spot my daughter emerging from a sea of kids. She looks hot and bothered. She opens the car door, plops down into the front seat and says: "Mom, you *know* you don't have to pick me up so early! Come later, when the traffic isn't so bad. I want to have time to talk with my friends!"

21

JUST ASSUME YOUR KIDS WILL OUTGROW YOU AND EVERYTHING WILL BE OKAY

When each of my daughters were born, I took pictures of our feet together. As newborns, their whole foot was as big as my big toe! When they were older, I used to kid them and ask: "When you outgrow those shoes will you hand them over to me?" I have small feet, and they had long passed me in the foot category. I could not even wear their hand me downs, which were expensive because they were practically new. Nowadays, by the time you have plunked down your $65.00 (this is the 1990's) for those "must have" sneakers and taken them home, your child has already outgrown them. It's the same way with clothes. So many times, I find myself asking my daughters: "What do you *mean* your jeans don't fit? We just bought that pair *yesterday!*"

What really drives me up the laundry shoot is the line: "Mom, I have nothing to wear!" My response: "Ever try looking in your closet?" When they can't find anything in their drawers and closets, they attack my drawers and closet. I figure my shoes are safe, but everything else is fair game.

They have worn my shirts, skirts, shorts, and pajamas. They can't quite fit into my jeans, so I'm still safe there. I guess they have done me a favor. Whenever I need anything, I can go see them. "Have you seen my white blouse with the V-neck?" I asked my younger daughter, Ashley. "Have you checked under my pillow?" she answers.

I usually can't wait for my birthday and Mother's Day to roll around because it is on those days when everyone in my family gives me clothes as presents. The excitement of opening the gift and seeing something new usually lasts five minutes, until one of my daughters will say: "Oh, Mom, that's cool! May I wear it sometime?"

I think that if I am patient, work my tail off at the gym, and maintain my minimum of four mouthfuls of food-on-the-run per day, I can keep my figure, and one day, get my clothes back. Since my daughters have outgrown me in the shoe department, and are fitting into most of my outfits now, by the time they go off to college they will be too big to take my clothes with them!

22

WHEN CHILDREN ARE NURTURING,
A MOM CAN REST

As moms, we think we have a monopoly on the nurturing gig. After all, we nurture our kids 24 hours a day, seven days a week. We nurture so much we forget to eat, sleep, get a manicure until softball season is over. Sometimes, however, there is an upside to this nurturing business.

"Mom, I know just what you need," said my then twelve-year-old daughter, Lindsay. She was referring to an upset stomach remedy that worked for her and she was sure it would work for me. I had over indulged on a steak the evening before.

I parked our car in front of the drugstore and watched her go in. A few minutes later she came out with a small bag and a smile on her face. She got back into the car. "Here Mom, this will help you," she said and took out some chewable tablets. "Oh, and I got you 7-Up, to help wash the medicine down."

I was just awestruck by her mature and caring attitude, but not totally surprised. Even when we think our children are not listening, they are listening. Even when we think they are not observing how we treat them and other people, they are observing. They have felt me hold them and console them with soft comforting words of love during those times when life seemed to be too much. They have felt such things as the stress of making new friends in a new school, and the sadness at their loss of childhood, as their bodies seemed to develop before their emotions.

In taking my daughter's remedies, she was asking something of me, to accept that she could be responsible. The ebb and flow of the separation tide can be tough sometimes. Our children struggle with growing up. We struggle with letting them go. The measure of our comfort level must depend on what we've said and done and perhaps how we've said and done it.

We picked up a pizza on the way home for her and her sister. When we got home, Lindsay got everything ready, served dinner to her sister, Ashley, and they plopped down in front of the television set to watch a movie. A half hour later, she asked: "Feeling better now, Mom?" "Yes," I told her. "I feel pretty incredible."

23

A DAY WITH MY DAUGHTER

(A COMBINATION OF MEMORIES WITH BOTH MY DAUGHTERS)

It is autumn in Mt. Kisco, New York. The afternoon breeze swirls the orange, red, yellow leaves on our path into mini funnels mixed with dust, as my two-year-old daughter and I take a walk in the woods. The chill in the air fills our lungs as we hunt for just the right leaves to take home with us, and dip into paraffin. As I walk with my daughter, she is all motion in her yellow sweater and blue corduroys and little blue sneakers. Her auburn curls touch her little shoulders and I want to bottle this day forever.

As we walk forward, she is suddenly eight years old and we are exploring tide pools around Half Moon Bay in California. We pick up seaweed, rocks, and seashells. We examine their textures and shapes. She asks me so many questions and I try to answer all of them with enthusiasm. At the same time, I wish she was still in my womb so I could protect her from the storms of life that will come, the waves of doubt and fear that will wash over her at times. That's just life.

As we walk forward our path is of a different nature today. We are at the mall, in Dallas, Texas, shopping. She wants to get her belly button pierced, at thirteen years old. She wants to try on makeup and look pretty. If she only knew how beautiful she is to me, just the way she is...my precious treasure.

I buy her a pair of jeans and a cute top. She is still so young. We share a pizza and drink sodas. We laugh together. And, I remember the days with my mom, when she took me to a restaurant for Chinese food and shopping at Rike's department store in downtown Dayton, Ohio. She bought me a *Barbie* doll when I was seven years old, the very first one made with the black and white striped bathing suit. She tried to explain why this *Barbie* was different from my other dolls. I just loved *Barbie*'s long black hair. I wanted to brush it all the time. I look at my daughter's hair as she asks me if I like it, "half-hair up," meaning, half of her hair is pulled out of her face. "Yes," I tell her. "You look so pretty!"

As we walk forward my daughter bounces down the stairs. It is 6:00 a.m. Her bags are packed for her trip to college. They sit like tombstones by the front door. Our taxi arrives. We hug each other with tears in our eyes. It is time to go.

On the airplane she lays her head in my lap and I stroke her hair as I gaze out the window at the mountains passing beneath us. They move as if in slow motion.

Time seems to pass slowly, but it is really travelling at the speed of light. The years slip rapidly away. Suddenly, my daughter is grown, off to college, and out of my life. I want to hold her forever and tell the world to leave us alone. This is my daughter. You can't have her. She's mine! But the plane keeps moving toward our destination, John Wayne Airport, in Orange, California.

As we walk forward, my daughter is sick with the flu. I take care of her in her apartment. My college student still needs her mom. So, I give her medicine and we watch a movie together, and I hold her again. As we walk forward it is Mother's Day. My daughter, now twenty years old, and I have brunch together in this coastal town called, La Jolla. Later, we shop for clothes. In the evening, we watch the sun set from our hotel room.

As we walk forward, I get a telephone call from my daughter. How did she get to be twenty-two years old? She says she is taking the day off. Do I want to come have fun with her and see a movie. I am there in a flash. The movie, that has a mother and daughter reconciling in it, makes us cry. We pass tissues to each other in the dark. After the movie, we get coffee and sit outside at this café on this brisk autumn day. The wind blows our hair as we sip our coffee. The wind blows us forward, as we hug each other goodbye, until next time, when I have a day with my daughter.

24

ANGELS ON THE HIGHWAY

M y daughter, Lindsay, calls and tells me, after the fact, that she helped a young woman rescue a big white dog on the Los Angeles 405 freeway during morning rush hour. After I pick my heart up off the floor, I ask her to tell me the details. "Well, Mom, someone just abandoned this sweet dog," she says. "He looked like he was part Labrador, part German Shepherd. I helped this girl put him in the back of her SUV. She was on her way to work, too. I told her I thought there was an animal shelter nearby. She was going to take the dog there. He made a mess in her SUV because he was so dirty, but at least we saved his life."

Ever since my daughters were born, I've prayed every day that God would surround them with His angels and protect them. Who knows how many times His angels have worked in both my daughters' lives, but I'm guessing it was, and continues to be, a lot.

Once, my younger daughter, Ashley, hit a brick wall along the tollway in Dallas, Texas with her car because a man turned his road rage onto her. She kept trying to get away from him and exit the tollway, but he kept coming around to stop her. He caused her car to spin around and around in the middle of the tollway and she crashed into the wall on the side of the tollway. Then, he sped away.

This was on a Friday night. Miraculously, no other cars appeared on the freeway for several minutes. Since her Jetta's car engine was built to "go under" the car on impact, it did not crush my daughter. She and her friends who were in the car had only minor scrapes and bruises. So, I thank God for His angels, who are always working overtime, I'm thinking, wherever we seem to go.

25

THE LAST ROAD TRIP WITH MY MOTHER
(DECEMBER 2010)

My mother, Carol, is eighty-four years old and very sprightly. I am, well, driving to Sacramento from the Los Angeles area so she can visit her eighty-six-year-old sister, Margie. They have not seen each other in three years and this might be the last time. It is Christmastime. This is my gift to my mother. We get caught in traffic, even though it is midmorning. We drive on. It begins to rain. The freeway gets wet and slippery.

We drive higher into the mountains on "The Grapevine." Suddenly, we are in a blinding blizzard. My mother keeps talking. I keep praying. We keep moving. The snow is so beautiful. It reminds me of the time my daughter, Ashley, four years old at the time, looked up into the snowflakes falling on our deck in our home near San Francisco and exclaimed: "Mommy! Look! It's a lizard!"

I finally get through "The Grapevine." My husband, Michael, calls me on my cell phone to tell me that I just made it. They just closed it.

Am I doing the same thing with my life, I wonder. If all my fears were snowflakes, I can aptly say that I sometimes feel like I'm in a blizzard. My mother will die someday. My kids might die. My husband might die. I could die without realizing all my dreams. How do I say, "yes," before God closes the door to "The Grapevine" of my life? How do I live my life with the blizzard swirling all around me?

My mother and I stop at this café. We sit at a table and drink our cups of hot, comforting coffee. I gaze at my mother's beautiful face and try to memorize her because I know this will be the last road trip we will ever take together. I am grateful for the several road trips we have done in our lives. I am grateful for the many road trips my mother planned for us as a family when I was a child. She was the "queen" of road trip planning. Have "trip-tic-will-travel," was her motto. And we did. We ventured to Cheyenne, Wyoming; Badlands National Park; the Adirondacks; so many road trips. But, I wonder, how many road trips do we not take because we are afraid, or do not make the time for?

I am glad I'm on this road trip with my mother. She tells me her jokes for the twentieth time. I laugh like I have heard them for the very first time. We see her sister, my Aunt Margie. My mother and aunt laugh together in this common living room area of this assisted living place, as they share stories of their childhood.

"Remember when you threw Doris' clothes up the attic stairs because she wouldn't hang them up?" asks my aunt, regarding their youngest sister.

"Remember when you beat that boy up because he called you a tomboy?" asks my mother, of her sister. They laugh and laugh. I am happy for them.

I gaze at the other women in the retirement home where my aunt lives. I try to imagine them as teenagers, so full of life. It is just their young spirits being held hostage in their old bodies. What did they do with their lives? What do they wish they could do now, if they could suddenly become young again and run out the door to take one last road trip?

On our drive home, my mother and I ramble leisurely through "The Grapevine." It is much warmer now. The snow has melted and the sun is setting ever so gently on the lush green hills of California. The sun's outstretched rays hug them like a loving mother hugs her child. I will miss this. I could drive forever watching the sun set on these hills with my mother.

26

VIEW FROM MY
GRANDDAUGHTER'S EYES
(NOVEMBER, 2021)

One of the biggest delights of my life is *Facetiming* with my grandkids, a grandson, Brock, who is seven years old, and granddaughter, Logan, almost four years old. Once a week, I read bedtime stories to my grandson, or he will read to me. I miss them so much as we live far apart, but with my grandson, we have a standing bedtime story date once a week and it is great.

My granddaughter's schedule is more flexible. My daughter, Ashley, picks her up at nursery school and brings her home for lunch. Today, we are eating our lunch together via *Facetime*. My little granddaughter is showing me a doll she bought with some money her kind hearted brother gave her. She is so proud of her little doll and all the accessories it comes with, like little shoes, dresses, and all. I listen with great intent because her little voice will not be little forever, so I want to capture and hold onto each moment as long as I can.

Logan and I want to chat more so my daughter gives her

the cell phone. Logan asks me: "Want to see my room?" I have seen it in person a hundred times, rocked her to sleep, changed her diapers, but of course, I say, yes. So, with cell phone in her little hands, I am seeing the ceiling, the drapes, her bed. Then, she shows me her jewelry box, her little necklaces, and her two lovely princess crowns on her dresser.

"These are my crowns," she says, in her sweet voice. I ask her to sing me her favorite song from the movie, *The Little Mermaid*. She sings and I listen, getting a bit teary eyed. I still remember taking my daughter, Ashley, to see that movie when she was four years old. Where did the time go? She loved everything mermaid. I even gave her a "Little Mermaid" party for her 19th birthday.

"Want to see my dresses?" asks my beautiful granddaughter. She shows me her pretty princess dresses, *Belle* and others. Soon, I am looking at the floor again. I think she is trying on one of her dresses to surprise me. All finished, she and I see each other again. She has on her gorgeous blue "Little Mermaid" gown. Such a lovely princess, just like her mama.

I tell her to take the cell phone down to her mom so she can take a picture of her. Again, I see the stairs, the ceiling, the floor, then her mom's face. A picture is taken and sent to me. We blow kisses and say our long goodbyes as my heart aches to hug them both. I look at my cell phone at the picture of my granddaughter, my precious little mermaid.

27

MAKING ROOM FOR THE NEW BABY
(DECEMBER 2021)

It was a whole domino effect. My oldest daughter, Lindsay, and her husband, Shawn, had to make room for their future baby, with crib, dresser, rocking chair in a room they were decorating for their child-to-be. So, they were having the movers bring their guest room bed to my house, plus two nightstand tables. Like I have the room!

Most of the "stuff" in my garage belongs to both my daughters. Okay, I'll admit it. Several of the boxes of stuff I have saved from when my kids were babies and children, that I just can't part with. I have things like their stuffed teddy bears, trolls, *Barbie* dolls, and yes, some baby teeth in a metal box shaped like a heart. "Don't send me those teeth!" my daughter, Ashley, says. "My kids still believe in the tooth fairy!" I have their special papers upon which they wrote their cute stories and poems, and some of their artwork. I have some of their baby clothes and shoes.

My oldest daughter and her husband barely have enough space for all the baby things for my future grandchild, but one of these days I am sending a moving pod to my younger daughter's residence. And, I still have some stuff from when I was a child, like my *Betsy Wetsy* doll, my *Betsy McCall* doll, my pink ragged eared elephant, and my brown teddy bear with part of an ear missing, when I, at three years old, tried to give him a haircut.

Some of the things I have are valuable, like my mother's hand carved wooden doll bed and doll trunk. You never know what you are going to find when you go on a "de-clutter" treasure hunt. I found a black and white picture of my high school senior graduating class. Everyone's picture was there in the shape of a tiny oval with their name under it. That was a lucky find, since my high school reunion is next year, and not to be unkind, but I might not recognize some people.

I called the *Got Junk* people and got rid of my old bed to make room for the new bed. I got rid of an old air conditioner. I called the *Vietnam Veterans Administration*, and got rid of three huge bags of clothes, some chairs, a cat bed and a rake. So, we are ready and waiting for the "new baby." I cannot wait to hold her in my arms and tell her stories about our family.

28

THE CIRCLE OF LIFE CONTINUES
(FEBRUARY 2022)

My third grandchild, Brynn, was born two weeks ago and she is a beauty. I had forgotten what holding a newborn felt like. It is sort of like holding a puppy. She is so small, with cute froggy legs, tiny arms, fingers, and toes. Another precious treasure is added to our family circle.

Newborn photos capture the moments of our lives: me holding her; my younger daughter, Ashley, holding her; my son-in-law, Shawn (her daddy) holding her, and my so very tired daughter, Lindsay (her mom) feeding her. We were all together celebrating this new life.

I'm so thankful I live only an hour away and will get to see this grandchild more often. When I lie in bed at night my heart always wanders to my family members. I feel like some mother hen without her brood. Then, my mind wanders to when I was a child, feeling safe and warm with my siblings and parents under one roof.

Then, my mind wanders to when my children were

teenagers. If they went out with their friends I couldn't rest until I knew they were home safe and sound.

Family members hold our hearts, especially new ones. It means we continue, as do some traditions that make us a family, no matter how far away we are from each other. I just now *Facetimed* with my younger daughter, Ashley, and my granddaughter, Logan, who is four years old. They are making banana bread. As they put all the ingredients into a big bowl and my granddaughter mixes the ingredients, I tell her stories about her great-grandma Carol's banana bread. My mom made the best. In fact, I am told they are using her special recipe.

I'll make my mom's banana bread this week and take it to my oldest daughter, a mother herself now. Someday, I will make banana bread for my youngest granddaughter. I will tell her stories, and as we smell the delicious smells coming from the oven, we will remember.

29

THERE'S NOTHING LIKE A GRANDSON TO TEACH YOU COURAGE

(MARCH, 2022)

"Come on, Mimi!" exclaims my grandson, Brock, seven years old. "It will be fun!" We are at a giant indoor waterpark in Sheboygan, Wisconsin. His father, Jeff, had encouraged him to go down the big waterslide a few weeks ago, so now he wants to encourage me. Going to an indoor waterpark and sliding down giant waterslides is what families do here, especially in the wintertime, when it is freezing outside. We get settled in our resort hotel, where everything is enclosed, like some giant greenhouse.

Dressed in our bathing suits, carrying our towels, water bottles, snacks, we get settled in our special spot by the biggest waterslide I have ever seen. Then, my daughter, Ashley, and my granddaughter, Logan, watch us, as Brock and I go up three flights of stairs to the very top of this waterslide. Together, Brock and I carry our big yellow tandem floating inner tube. Now, mind you, I am a person who really does not like the water. I like to sit by water. I like to go kayaking in it. But, dunk my head. No way!

We keep climbing up the three flights of stairs and finally make our way to the very top. A man standing guard for our safety, helps us get into our inner tube situated at the top of the slide. Oh boy, am I nervous! What if we get stuck, I wonder. How deep is the water at the bottom? What if we tip over?

"One-two-three go!" my grandson shouts. We push off with our arms and away we go! We are flying, as we zip down the curvy slide. We are zigging. We are zagging. We move this way and that, so fast it makes my head spin! It is an exhilarating feeling that makes me instantly feel like a child again. "Yipee!" my heart is shouting, as my mind forgets what day and year it is. We go underneath a waterfall and get our hair wet. How refreshing! Did time carry me away to a tropical paradise for two seconds? Soon, our ride is over, and I am feeling disappointed. I want to be a child again, I think, as we wash out into a pool and begin drifting.

Wow, that was not bad at all. It was a lot of fun! My daughter filmed the whole thing on her cell phone, getting such a kick out of watching her mother going down a water-slide at my age. Of course, she is laughing with joy that her mom had such a great time laughing and fun "screaming," the whole way down.

My granddaughter is laughing, too. My grandson and I look at each other and he smiles at me. It is a smile I will never forget. As I am thinking I am too old for this waterslide business, he encourages me once more.

"Mimi, let's go again with our own inner tubes!" he says. "I'll race ya!" "Okay, you're on!" I reply. And, off we go!

30

BABYSITTING MY TODDLER GRANDDAUGHTER
(FEBRUARY 2023)

My daughter, Lindsay, asked if I would babysit my thirteen-month-old granddaughter, Brynn, for the weekend, and of course, I said, yes. She and my son-in-law, Shawn, wanted to take a trip together. The gift of time, whether it be with family or friends, is always at the top of my list. To be able to give that gift to my daughter and her husband gave me joy. And, I had the whole weekend to play with my granddaughter.

I was with Brynn all day on Friday. My daughter and her husband left the house after my granddaughter went to sleep for the night on Thursday. Then, it was all me, until Monday morning. So, on Saturday morning, Brynn woke up at 6:30 a.m. and we played for nearly twelve hours, except for her hour or so nap in the afternoon. I put her into her huge playpen, and we played puzzles and put the nesting cups together.

Then, we played, "Mimi-catch-the-balls-I-throw-out-onto-the floor." I must say, she has got quite a throwing arm from her playpen! We sang songs. We played, "where's Mimi?" For this game, I put her into her walker and hide in the kitchen. She's like, "Rambo," now in her walker and is quick to find me. Then, I run over to the front door and hide behind the wall and she's "Rambo," again. This goes on for about ten minutes.

At meal times, I put her into her high chair and she watches me pretend to be "Super Chef," as I heat up her veggies and meats on the stove at lunch and dinner and make her scrambled eggs or oatmeal at breakfast. Later, I take her for walks in her stroller, and we explore the different flowers and say hello to various dogs and people. She loves to wave at everyone and they smile back at her and sometimes people comment. They say: "Did you see that baby? She's waving at us!"

Brynn is the happiest baby ever. The only time she cries is when she's teething or misses mommy and daddy, which was only one night. She was giggling as a newborn and still laughs a lot. It makes us all laugh, even though we have no idea what she is laughing about.

Bedtime is 6:30. I get her into her pajamas. We read stories. She likes the stories about hippos or dinosaurs. I, of course, make all the funny noises and she laughs. Then, I put her into her sleep sack. I hold her and we turn out the lights and I sing lullabies to her. Since it's the first time her mommy and daddy are not there, I sing her a few extra songs, as I hold her, and walk back and forth across the room. And, I feel like a young mommy again.

It all goes by too fast, as I remember holding my daughters and singing to them when they were small. As I walk with my granddaughter and sing to her in the dark, she rests her little head on my shoulder and I am in Heaven.

31

BEING RIGHT VERSES A SIBLING'S LOVE

I cannot imagine my life without my awesome brothers, Dan and John, and wish I could see them more often. Who else but our siblings remember the times we went sled riding down our hill and piled the snow way up high because we thought it would be fun to "fly through the air?"

Who else can I share the memories of us telling stories in our secret clubhouse with our dad's huge tape recorder? We recorded our stories in our mom's pantry in our "mudroom." The tape recorder looked like a huge box with two tape-recording wheels on top about five inches in diameter. I wish I had those tapes today of the stories we told with a flashlight in the dark.

Who else can I laugh with at the time, Taffy, our Golden Retriever, snatched a whole ham off our kitchen table that our mom was preparing for dinner? We could tell by the trail of grease around the corner of the kitchen who the culprit was, and laughed and laughed, though our mother was not happy.

We share a lifetime with our siblings unless the chain of love is broken. Misunderstandings, unyielding wills, power struggles, past hurts, can surely separate us from each other, for months or years at a time. I think back to when my oldest brother, Dan, almost died from a drug overdose when doctors put him under for what they said, was a simple tonsillectomy. After praying throughout the night, with my mom and her friends, Dan woke up after 24 hours, and was okay.

And, I remember when my younger brother, John, was close to having his appendix burst when he was in college. I believe angels were watching over him that night, as the doctors got to him just in time.

I know friends who have lost their siblings through death and would do anything to get them back. I know friends who have lost their siblings by not talking to them for years while they are still walking this earth. Time is promised to no one.

Lost time is love lost. Family ties can bind and gag us, as my friend, Erma Bombeck once wrote, but forgiveness is a short string back home.

32

SOMETHING ABOUT SISTERS

I never had a sister, but if I did, she would be my cousin, Louise. Her mom, my Aunt Margie, and my mom, Carol, were best friends. They would talk for hours on the telephone and laugh like crazy. They have both passed away, but the memories live on, especially when Louise and I now talk on the telephone and laugh like crazy.

Several years ago, I drove my mom from the Los Angeles area to Sacramento to see her sister for the last time. Margie was in an assisted living facility, but smart as a whip, as was my mom. They spent a delightful afternoon one winter before Christmas, reminiscing about their childhood. The last words my aunt said to her sister before we had to leave was: "See you on the other side." I suspect now, they are both laughing in Heaven.

I always sort of envied the bond some sisters have, but feel so blessed that my daughters, Lindsay, and Ashley, have that bond. I always reminded them growing up of the dear friendship their grandma and great aunt had together, and hoped that my daughters would be best friends.

They are, but it didn't start out that way. I think friendships between siblings have to be nurtured by the parents. When Ashley was born, Lindsay was two-and-a-half. She was used to being the center of attention and didn't like this new addition to our family at first. Once, when we were driving in the car, Ashley began crying. As I was trying to console my newborn, my toddler suddenly blurted out: "Ashley, stop crying! It's *my turn* to cry!"

Although they have had their ups and downs, they had fun times together. They loved to dress up in their ballet tutus and perform together; play in the sandbox with their bunny, Fluffy, and see who could soar the highest in their swings in the backyard. They enjoyed feeding their ducks, Daisy and Maisy, racing their pet lizards, and holding their umbrellas high up on the backyard hill during a rain storm to play, "Mary Poppins!"

During their teenage years, since their voices sounded alike, they loved fooling their boyfriends when answering the telephone. When their bedrooms looked like they got hit by a tornado, they would turn on music, clean their rooms and proudly prove to me that I didn't have to shut their doors forever. In college, they got to spend one year together, when Lindsay was a senior and Ashley was a freshman. They had their own friends and parties, and lives, but looking back, I think they wish they had spent more time together.

Lately, they are getting to see each other more than expected. When Lindsay had to have a major surgery, Ashley was her nurse, always by her side. Their bond is closer than ever. They have taken some fun trips together, and now, as mothers of daughters, I like to think that "their daughters," will carry on the legacy. Cousins, Logan and Brynn, will be devoted to each other. Ashley and Lindsay will see to that. But there is nothing like a sister bond.

33

THE SUMMER MY FATHER WENT OFF TO FIGHT IN A WAR

I t was July 16, 1944, when my father, Joseph F. Accrocco, went off to fight in WWII in the South Pacific. After weeks of training, he was now a proud Marine in the United States Marine Corps. He was given a leave of two weeks prior to being shipped out to visit with family members and friends in Ohio, to tell them he loved them and to say good-bye. He did not know if he would be coming home again. It was a bittersweet visit.

He was young, at age twenty-four, not knowing what was ahead. His battalion, the 29th Engineering Battalion of 300-500 men boarded a train at Camp Lejeune train depot to head west to San Diego. There, he would board a ship that would embroil him on a journey no man should have to take, but he wanted to go, to fight for his country.

As I sit enjoying the warm evening sunset on my porch in July, 2022, I think of him. He is riding the train across the plains of America. The Marines slept ten men to a Pullman car, bathrooms at either end, a kitchen in the middle. They brought their sea bags with clothing and personal gear.

As the train engine hissed, they formed ranks and boarded the Pullmans. One-hundred-thirteen thousand special troop trains transported around 44 million members of the military from the time of Pearl Harbor, to June 1945. The men were fed basic but hearty meals of baked ham, boiled potatoes, bread, cooked greens that reminded them of their mothers' cooking back home. They played cards, read, and watched the scenery go by from their train car windows.

Fleeting views of families having dinner in their track-side homes brought waves of homesickness for some of these young men. Brief stops boosted their spirits as people along their route waved American flags, cheering them on their way to fight for our freedom. Mothers brought baskets of food. The Salvation Army volunteers offered their thanks with gifts of coffee and donuts.

As the train chugged across the plains of our great country, they saw the night sky filled with stars. And, the sunrises and sunsets brought such beauty the Marines had never seen before, going off to war. On the train they laughed and joked, told stories, showed pictures of their girlfriends or family members. They tried hard to stuff their fears of the unknown that lay ahead like dark shadows. They traveled through Texas in the terrific heat. Stops meant time for one-hour calisthenics ordered by the Colonel. Some stops included nicer meals at restaurants.

I imagine my father savored the scenes of rolling plains stretching as far as the soul could breathe. He thought it must be the most beautiful land on the face of the earth, America. The train chugged on...winding through Winslow and Flagstaff, Arizona; to Needles and Barstow, California; then down to San Bernardino, Riverside, Orange and finally to San Diego. They arrived on July 21, 1944, a Saturday. I wish I could have seen my father's face when he saw the blue Pacific Ocean for the first time. Knowing my father's tender heart, it must have astonished him to see such beauty, as he pushed back his fears and tried to strengthen his faith.

The Marines got a one-day leave, a final farewell in their country and a taste of freedom. They listened and danced to bands at Jimmy Kennedy's New Paris Inn. I saw a photo once of my father with his fellow Marines at a table there. They are smiling, so happy, so innocent. My dad, Joe, is with his best friend, Jack. They had been trained, but they had no idea of the horrors of war that would take away their innocence and the lives of friends they knew.

All too soon my father's battalion left on the *SS Mormacsea*. The rest of the battalion that included Jack, left on *The USS Morton*. There is a picture of the two ships heading out to sea, at sunset. *The USS Morton* is following the *SS Mormacsea*, in the summer of 1944, full of brave men, who fought for the freedom of our country, going off to war.

(Information courtesy of *O'er The Ramparts He Watched: Memoir of a Pacific Marine*, by Daniel Joseph Accrocco.)

PART III

THE SEASONS OF OUR LIVES

34

A SUMMER'S DAY AT THE BEACH
(2017)

I went back to one of my old haunts today, Manhattan Beach, California. The wide stretch of clean sand, sparkling blue water that meets the sky, and waves that race like white horses to shore when they crest and foam, gave new breath to my soul. It was a sunny day, 72 degrees, as the rays warmed me and the gently blowing breezes comforted me. I thanked God for leading me here.

This peaceful place was my home for a year after my soul was broken but free, an emotional wreck like the seaweed washed ashore, tangled but intact. It was where my dog, Charley, and I walked along The Strand, where I made new friends, where I found the "person" I had lost so many years ago...me.

It was where I fell in love again. And it is where, after several years of spending many lovely days by the ocean together, I took my love, my husband, Michael, to see one last time before he died. I come back to the ocean not so much to remember but to keep moving forward as I watch the waves ebb and flow. They are timeless, yet hold secrets of the centuries in all the memories here.

What is it about the ocean that makes it feel like home and tugs at our hearts? I once asked a friend: "When do all the sad memories go away?" And she replied: "When you make new, good memories." I worked on that notion and have done okay over the years, since becoming a widow, but I do not necessarily think sad memories wash away like footprints in the sand. I think the waves wash us new again, in spite of them.

35

LAST TIME I LOOKED I WAS 29

I am standing at the top of the stairs in the Main Concourse in Grand Central Terminal in Midtown Manhattan, New York City. It is June, muggy in 1983. I am about eight months pregnant with my first child, Lindsay, wearing a maternity dress, my *Anne Klein* heels, having just gotten out of a meeting with the editor-in-chief and our team of writers at *Bride's*.

I am holding my briefcase in one hand and resting my other hand on top of my big belly. As I am looking down at all the people scrambling to catch their trains home, I am thinking about my child-to-be and how I can protect her from the world. It can be cruel sometimes.

I have one more month to write the honeymoon chapter of a book we are all putting together, a celebration of fifty years of *Bride's*. There was a delay with the publishers, so, instead of our book being written already, I am guessing I will be writing my chapter as I go into labor and beyond.

Yes, that is what happened. I wrote until the labor pains

made it impossible to write anymore. I kept thinking of the words in my head as my trusty dog, Sunny, walked with me back and forth across our family room floor. Funny, thinking about it, how my beloved dog would pace with me like that. He was all the company I had until, thank goodness, my then husband's train coming from Manhattan was not delayed getting to the Mt. Kisco station near our home.

My mother was there to help me with my baby, my Lindsay, after she was born, as I continued to write, nurse her, and write some more. To have a book and a baby come out, though not at the same time, made me feel very productive. So, why am I telling you this story? I think it is because as my "umpteenth" birthday approaches, I feel 29 again. Years ago, I felt like I was 80 years old, when I was dealing with many trials and could not see the light at the end of the tunnel.

But through persevering, by God's grace, I got to the light. I got out of the tunnel. And, now it feels like I am surrounded by all the good memories in a happy life with my many friends and wonderful family members. I am once again standing at the top of the stairs looking down at the world. People are frantically scattering everywhere under the pressure of possibly missed trains.

I may have missed a few trains myself, but I have never stopped dreaming, from trying, from hoping that I still can have beautiful things to see and things to do. If I don't quit; if "we" don't quit, we can't miss the train.

36

AGE IS THE NUMBER OF WISDOM

My birthday is coming up soon and I am not dreading it, although I wish it was a smaller number. I think we all wish that, unless you are thirty years old right now, and good for you. If I could choose a number or time in my life where I felt most young and free it would be when I was twenty years old, summer, England, 1975.

I had the opportunity to spend most of the summer at Trinity College, Oxford University. I studied Shakespeare and art. A group of us students sat with our dons in lovely gardens and had intellectual discussions about so many wonderful things.

In August, after our classes were over, we had the chance to travel. So, with my backpack and *Eurail* pass I boarded a train for the Cotswolds. I was a skinny kid in those days. I think my backpack weighed as much as me. As I stood in the train car aisle looking for a seat, the train lunged forward and I fell backwards onto my backpack in the aisle! Several people laughed. Not to be deterred, I rolled onto my side, picked myself up and finally found a seat. People were mostly nice. I guess I made their day with laughter.

I stayed quite happily in a bed and breakfast with a window view of a hundred sheep on the green hillsides by a babbling brook. A cheerful couple, the owners, treated me like their daughter. I was on my own and loved it.

I hiked all over the place, sat at tables with welcoming locals and talked for hours with them. How I wished I could have stayed in my own little cottage and written poems to my heart's content. But one thing about life is, it keeps pushing us forward. So, what can we learn about life? What has it taught us? How many candles on our birthday cakes do we have to blow out to appreciate the wisdom all those years gave us, whether we wanted all those years or not?

My wisdom is not the same as yours. But after all the heartbreaks, the laughter, the tears, the one thing I do know is this: I am happy to be alive and grateful for each new day. I am happy when I can share good thoughts and wisdom with my grandson, Brock, and stories about my life. Though he may not remember, I tell him things about his great-grandpa Joe, and great-grandma, Carol.

I tell him about the time the Ohio River flooded and how his great-grandpa, Joe, rowed people across the river in his rowboat when he was fourteen years old. I tell him how his great-grandma, Carol, when she was a child and living in Rochester, New York, went to church in a car that had no heat. She and her siblings had to cover themselves in the backseat with a Buffalo hide blanket to keep warm. Her mother, great-great grandma, Helen, would warm bricks in the oven, then cover them with a towel, to warm everyone's feet when they sat in the car with no heat, on their way to church.

I figure some things are worth sharing. And, maybe one day, my grandkids will tell their kids. So, from my perspective, I do not much mind getting older. Just don't make my cake look like a bonfire!

37

AUTUMN

I take walks in my little historic town. Even though we do not have an amazing colorful autumn as in other parts of our country, we have maple trees, whose leaves are now turning orange and red against a soft blue California sky. There are pumpkins on mostly everyone's porch. Many of our town folk have quite a sense of humor and a love for harvest time.

There are skeletons having an elegant dinner on a lawn nearby. Other skeletons are climbing on rooftops of the local pubs pretending to be pirates. Store windows display sweaters, skirts, and boots. The antique shops host an array of harvest teacups and plates, assorted decorations. And the local restaurants entice me with the aromas of pumpkin spice lattes, pumpkin muffins, and pumpkin waffles.

When I was a student at Ohio University, I entered the *Mademoiselle* Guest Editor Competition. The contest rules were that one had to write about a fun weekend getaway. So, I grabbed my friend who was a photographer, got my reporter's writing pad, and went to the Circleville Pumpkin festival in Circleville, Ohio, to interview farmers and other participants.

The farmers were very proud of their pumpkins that were as big as boulders, and gourds as big as guitars. I had never seen so many "things pumpkin," in my whole life. They even had pumpkin taffy and pumpkin fudge.

When I was a child, my brothers, Dan and John, and our friends used to play in Groby's Field, near our house. Mr. Groby, who owned a local fruit and vegetable market in town, always left us some pumpkins and gourds around harvest time. And, the store owners at our local shopping center always let us paint their windows with scenes of pumpkins.

But of all the memories and traditions I love the most, was when my parents took us hiking in Hueston Woods near our home in Dayton, Ohio. The colors of the leaves were so beautiful, and the calming scent of the autumn leaves crunching beneath our feet is forever etched in my mind.

Autumn is a time for slowing down, taking a deep breath, and reminding ourselves that life still offers joyful moments. Whether it is a latte at a table in the sun with a good book, or finally getting to wear a favorite sweater, autumn offers lots of pumpkins.

38

AUTUMN, PART TWO

As was tradition in our family, my mother would begin baking when the leaves began to fall and we would get that first "chill" in the air. She loved to bake sugar cookies, cowboy cake, and strawberry jelly tarts. And, I liked to bake bread. Not too long ago, I took out my grandmother Helen's leather-bound cookbook of treasured family recipes written in her own handwriting.

There was no date on my grandmother's recipe book, but she used butter, lard, shortening and real sugar in those days. As I perused recipes, such as "Johnny Cake," "Orange Marmalade Muffins," and "Minced Meat Pie," I settled on one recipe that looked interesting. Among the "Pickled Beets," and "Cream Puff" recipes, there was "Molasses Holiday Hermits."

I have no idea why the "Hermit," title, but it looks good: ¾ cup shortening, ¼ cup sugar, 1 egg, 1 cup molasses, 3 cups sifted all-purpose flour, 2 teaspoons baking powder, 1 teaspoon each of cinnamon and ginger, ½ teaspoon salt, 1 cup dried candied fruit.

Cream shortening and sugar. Blend in egg and molasses. Add sifted dry ingredients. Mix well. Stir in raisins, nuts, and dried fruit. Drop rounded teaspoonfuls of this mixture onto a greased cookie sheet. Bake in moderate oven at 350 degrees for 15 minutes. This makes sixty cookies.

I think I'll make these cookies soon. They would go well with a cup of hot tea, as I wistfully dream of "sweater weather."

39

HALLOWEEN IS ALMOST UPON US

"We weren't sure if you were a trick or a treat!" my mom would tell me, regarding the day I was born. Then, she would laugh and say: "Nah, you're a treat!" It was fun being a "close enough" Halloween baby, as I got to have birthday costume parties, and pumpkin shaped cakes that were usually chocolate inside. All my friends who were invited to my party got to bash a piñata pumpkin with a baseball bat and grab all the candy that fell to the ground!

I remember going trick-or-treating the first time at age five, in my silk purple and gold costume. I was "Snow White," and my dad who held my hand went as, "Dad." For those of you who might be interested, trick-or-treating began back in Scotland and Ireland in the 16th century and was called, "guising." People would go from house to house in costumes, put on small performances, and be rewarded with assorted treats.

One year, I was a pilgrim. My brother, Dan, was "Huckleberry Hound," and my brother, John, was a skeleton in a black silk full body costume. My friend, Mary, and I were Beatniks when we were ten, and carried pillow cases instead of small bags, to get more candy. "Haven't we seen you two before?" my three spinster sister neighbors asked when we were being a little naughty and went to the same house twice.

As a grown up, I attended my girlfriend Heidi's big Halloween costume party in a red lacy dress because I had a figure like *Barbie*, back then. By day, I was the matronly dressed volunteer at my kids' elementary school. One year, my two daughters, Ashley and Lindsay, were dressed up as ballerinas. The excitement of the two of them, ages four and six-and-a-half, running from house to house as their pink and blue tutus bounced up and down as they ran, will forever be etched in my memory. Another fun memory is of my daughter, Lindsay, dressed as a "granny," bobbing for apples at her fourth grade Halloween party. All the kids were getting their faces wet, but not her! She simply bent down and picked up an apple by the stem! I thought that was genius!

In my current town, Halloween is a big deal. We have a Halloween decorating contest, so orange lights and elaborate decorations are displayed on almost every house. We have a giant "Stay Puff Marshmallow Man," cornstalks and haystacks, climbing skeletons, and witches stuck in trees. And, we always have that "one neighbor," whose home looks like a cross between *Cirque du Soleil* and Tim Burton's, *Corpse Bride*.

And, we have lots of kids, who dress up as *Beatlejuices*, *Barbies*, and *Top Gun Maverick* pilots. I love seeing the

Minions, and mermaids who always say, "thank you," when I drop candy into their bags.

All is exciting and calm around here on Halloween night. At least, I hope it will stay that way. But frankly, I cannot wait for my, *The Burbs,* neighbor at the end of my street to take down his "monster-and-clown circus" and decorate for Christmas.

40

NEVER MET A TURKEY I DIDN'T LIKE

I f you have never seen the movies, *Christmas Vacation* or *The Money Pit*, I highly recommend them, especially the scenes with the turkeys. In *Christmas Vacation*, as the character, Clark Griswold, played by Chevy Chase, cuts into the turkey, with all the family members salivating around the table in hungry anticipation, it explodes! Literally.

Everyone decides to eat it anyway as they chomp on pieces of turkey guaranteed to tear out your dentures. In the movie, *The Money Pit*, Anna Crowley, played by Shelley Long, happily waits for her prized turkey to be done and it was more than...as it shoots out of the oven, breaks through a window and lands in the upstairs porcelain bathtub!

As Walter Fielding, played by Tom Hanks, and Anna watch for a few seconds in shock, the turkey and bathtub fall through the floor and crash onto the downstairs floor below! The bathtub breaks into a million pieces and the turkey is no more. Tom Hanks laughs so hysterically for about five minutes that I thought I was finally going to get "abs" from laughing so hard!

In real life, my former relatives accidentally set their turkey on fire and almost their house trying to barbecue it. My oldest daughter, Lindsay, had the foresight to film the whole thing. "Oh, *no*, the turkey is *ruined*!" lamented her Uncle Sam. "No, it's *not*," replied her Aunt Lisa. "Just brush off the charcoal parts!"

The best story is how Lindsay met her husband, Shawn. During another Thanksgiving, the whole family was in the dining room, waiting for dessert. Lindsay's Aunt Lisa was in the kitchen with Lisa's next-door neighbor, Evonne, Shawn's mother. As they were preparing the dessert, in walks Shawn through the front door, straight into the kitchen to see his mother.

Ashley immediately gets up and makes a beeline into the kitchen, introduces herself to Shawn and says: "You *have* to meet my sister!" He is thinking, yeah right. She can't be that cute if you are so desperate for me to meet her. But Shawn takes one look at Lindsay and Lindsay takes one look at Shawn and it is love at first sight!

Dessert is served, but Lindsay is disappointed that her aunt forgot to get pumpkin pie. A couple days later, Shawn flies back to Kansas City. Lindsay flies back to Los Angeles. The next day, there is a "knock" on Lindsay's door. She answers it. There is a delivery man with a box for her. "I didn't order anything," she says. He makes a telephone call and says: "Yes, this is for you!" She takes the box, thanks the delivery man, closes the door. She opens the box and it is a piece of pumpkin pie, from Shawn!

Three years later, during their wedding ceremony, Lindsay's final words to her beloved husband, Shawn, were: "You had me at pumpkin pie!"

41

WHO IS THIS "ELF ON THE SHELF?"

I was getting my hair done the other day and my hairdresser, Nicole, was lamenting about having to get up very early to move the "elf" to a different place in her house because she forgot to move him the night before. "What's that?" I asked. "You know, *The Elf on the Shelf*," she replied. "I have no idea," I answered.

She proceeds to tell me this whole story about this tradition with little kids that began in 2005. Apparently, a mother, Carol Aebersold, and her daughter, Chandra Bell, started it with a book, which has exploded into dolls, kits, accessories, pets, movies and more. The initial book comes with a "Scout Elf," that is either a boy or girl. As the story goes, which, if I was a kid, I would not want that "thing," in my house, watching my every move, but this little green elf comes to your house.

He takes over your house for the month of December and watches your children, who love this, apparently, to make sure if you are being naughty or nice. Your kids or grandkids can name them, but they can never touch them, or the elves will lose their magic. The elf comes to your home from the North Pole during "Scout Elf Return Week," usually November 24th through December 1st, to help Santa keep tabs on the kids' behavior on his "naughty and nice" list.

The elf sits in a certain spot during the day and returns to the North Pole at night to report to Santa. When Santa arrives on Christmas Day to deliver presents, the elf then returns to the North Pole for another year. The kids take delight in naming their elves, like Buddy or Winky or Hoppity. Or if you want to stick with Christmas themes, there's Snowy or Frosty. Personally, I would name my elf, "Snitch!"

The real work is on the parents, who must move the elf every night to a new place in the house so the kids can see he or she has moved by morning. Heaven help the poor parents if the family dog gets a hold of it and thinks it is a toy! One Christmas, my daughter, Ashley, received an interesting gift from her mother-in-law, Cathy. It was a Christmas fairy that looked a little scary.

My daughter and her husband, Jeff, named it, "Creepy-the-Freaky-Fairy." As a joke, each family member gets a turn to put "Creepy" somewhere. Sometimes "Creepy" appears beside the bed when you wake up or by the bathroom sink. There is the initial: "Oh, my gosh!" And, everyone laughs.

Christmas offers a lot of traditions, games, and fun, but when it all comes down to it, give me the "Star" on my Christmas tree, and baby "Jesus," in the manger.

42

CHRISTMASTIME MEANS COZY CHATS BY A FIRE

Not long ago, I met a dear girlfriend of mine, Kathy, at this restaurant in Hollywood, California, that used to be an old Spanish mission. As I walked through the huge iron gate I felt transported back in time. Since I was the first patron of the day, the kind hostess welcomed me to the best table in the house by a cozy fire burning slowly in a huge stone fireplace.

Kathy arrived, and soon we were sipping our hot coffees and eating chocolate croissants by the fire. The hectic pace of the approaching Christmas holiday season melted away, as we were reminded of what *really* mattered: friendly chats with old friends, future reunions with family members, singing Christmas carols and remembering the "reason for the season."

I do not know about you, but it seems that each year the holiday season seems to gain more speed. We just get busier, and we forget so much. I remember years ago, the excite-

ment my brothers and I felt as we waited in anxious anticipation for the Christmas television specials to air at certain
scheduled times. I remember making Christmas cookies
with our mother, going out as a family to find just the right
Christmas tree, and setting up our traditional wooden
manger.

Rike's department store in my hometown of Dayton,
Ohio, on the corner of Second and Main Streets, had incredible window displays, called, "The Rike's Winterland
Wonderland Windows," with puppets, music, animated
figures. Originally a Charles Dickens' theme of "A Christmas
Carol," it expanded to include a mom hanging an ornament
on a tree, bears on a teeter-totter, a dad rocking back and
forth playing a trumpet, elves, and reindeer prancing on the
roof through evergreen trees! My mother dressed us up and I
remember wearing my special Christmas dress, tights, and
black shiny patent shoes. After visiting Santa Claus and
shopping for little presents for our parents, they took us to
this Chinese restaurant where we learned to eat with
chopsticks.

My brother, John, wished for a *Bop a Bear*. My brother,
Dan, I think, wanted a plastic ranch with fences, horses, and
cowboys he could set up. I wanted a doll that looked like a
real baby. My parents, not wealthy by any means, made our
wishes come true on Christmas morning, but more than
that, they gave us love.

What I remember the most, was sled riding down hills of
white powdery snow, building snowmen in our backyard,
getting into our car to tour the houses in our area decorated
with the most beautiful red and green Christmas lights.

Later, we would go back home and our mom would serve us hot cocoa by a warm cozy fire flickering in our fireplace. Time seemed to mellow down, as we got sleepy watching the embers slowly burning, before going off to bed.

43

A CHRISTMAS LOVE STORY

I do not know if many of you remember the beautiful short story by O. Henry called, *The Gift of The Magi*, first published in 1905. Though movies have been made of this beautiful story, it got buried somewhere, among the comedies, *Home Alone*, and *Christmas Vacation*. While loads of fun, it is nice to slow down and remember what this season is about, God's love for us and for each other, about being kind.

As the story goes, there was a couple who were deeply in love named, Della, the wife, and her husband, Jim. Despite being very poor they had two treasures in their possession. Della had her gorgeous knee length brown hair, and Jim had a gold pocket watch, a family heirloom.

Unbeknownst to the two of them, Della so wanted to buy Jim a present for Christmas, that she sold her hair to buy Jim a platinum fob chain to go with his watch. Jim so wanted to buy Della a Christmas present that he sold his watch to buy Della a set of ornamental combs for her hair. On Christmas day they exchanged gifts.

Della opens her present of combs, as she assures Jim, with tears in her eyes, that her hair will grow back. Jim opens his gift of the watch chain, as he tells her that he sold his watch to buy her the combs. It is then they both realize how far they went to show their love for one another and how valuable their love truly was. The story of the Magi, as author O. Henry wrote, is that when people sacrifice their material possessions for the people they love, this is true wisdom, for they are as wise as the Magi.

There is another love story I would like to share about my mother, Carol, who lived in Silver Spring, Maryland, during WWII. When she was a young single woman, she went to visit her sister, Margie, on the train, to New York City. It was Christmastime, and she received a message from her mother, Helen, that Jim, an old soldier boyfriend, was able to get leave to come home for Christmas. He was going to be at Union Station in Washington DC, at the same time my mom was going to be at the station coming home from New York City. They met for one brief special moment on a wintry afternoon, and my mom mentioned how handsome he looked in his uniform.

Jim went back to Germany to fight in the war. My mother got on with her life working as a secretary typing memorandums for President Franklin D. Roosevelt. Jim married and moved to Florida. My mom married my dad, Joe, and we had a happy family life. Years later, Jim's wife died from cancer. My dad died from Alzheimer's disease. Somehow, Jim found my mother's address and they became pen pals for many years, never forgetting to send each other Christmas and birthday cards, as their fondness for each other grew. They never did see each other again, so they were "forever young," in each other's hearts and minds.

When my mom passed away, on April 27, 2016, being the one to remember everyone's birthday, she had a birthday card already addressed to Jim. I was the one who added a note to my mom's sweet words, to let Jim know that she passed away, and sent the card to him. As I put the card into the mailbox, with tears in my eyes, I thought to myself: I will never forget what a "gift" love is, at any age, especially at Christmas.

44

NEW YEAR'S RESOLUTIONS VERSES "DO OVERS"

F ew people probably remember the 1991 movie, *City Slickers*, starring Billy Crystal, Jack Palance, Daniel Stern, Bruno Kirby, with supporting roles by Patricia Wettig, Helen Slater, Noble Willingham, and Jake Gyllenhaal in his debut. It is an American comedy western about three friends going through a midlife crisis in their late 30's, early 40's.

After escaping their emotions on previous "guy" adventures like the "running of the bulls," in Pamplona, Spain, they decide, this particular year, to go on a cattle drive from New Mexico to Colorado.

Mitch Robbins, played by Billy Crystal, hates his advertising sales job. Phil Berquist, played by Daniel Stern, hates his grocery store manager job and his overbearing wife. She ends up divorcing him when he has an affair with a store clerk. And, Bruno Kirby, played by Ed Furillo, has a gorgeous model wife, but is scared to death of further commitment, like having children.

Barbara Robbins, played by Patricia Wettig, is sick of her

husband, Mitch, acting like the whole world barfed all over him. She tells him to get out of town, basically, and find his smile again, if he can. Mishaps and conflicts abound, starting with Mitch setting the cattle off on a stampede and destroying their campsite as he scares the herd grinding beans for his morning coffee. The guys are feeling lost, but trail boss, Curly Washburn, played by Jack Palance, is the wise old sage who gives them some advice. Just find that "one thing," in life that is important to you, he tells them. "What's that?" Mitch asks Curly. "That's what you've got to figure out," Curly replies.

Later, during a very frustrating moment, Phil explodes in anger. "I'm forty years old and I've wasted my life!" he tells Mitch. Suddenly, a light bulb goes on in Mitch's head as he tells Phil: "Yeah, but now ya got a chance to start over. Your life is a "do over.' You got a clean slate!"

How many of us wish we could just have a "do over," as opposed to making New Year's resolutions that make us feel like failures if we do not live up to them? Perhaps, if we focus on that "one thing," that is most important to us, we can give ourselves a "do over."

What is *your* one thing? Last year, my one thing, my "word," was "blossom." God gave me a jump start via a friend who told me to focus on the one thing that brings me joy. That joy is my writing. Using the gift God gave me to bless others. In blessing others, I feel I have gotten my "do over." My word this year, my one thing, is being "fearless." I am determined to knock all the fear obstacles out of my way and keep charging forward.

"So much of our life can be stolen by dwelling on fearful imaginations," said a man named, Ray Leight. And, another very wise man by the name of Pastor Chuck Smith, once said: "Everything is preparation for something else." So, what if all the bad things, all the hard things, the things that almost broke us, could be woven into a quilt of our wiser, more courageous lives, and made new again? What if we did give ourselves a "do over?"

45

ALL'S QUIET ON THE SNOWY FRONT: JANUARY 2024

Sixteen inches of snow fell in Wisconsin just before I arrived to babysit my grandkids. The temperature is thirty-three degrees now. This is a heat wave compared to the cool eleven degrees that chilled the air prior to my visit. But, wow, the snow! As J.B. Priestly once said: "The first fall of snow is not only an event but it is a 'magical event.' You go to bed in one kind of world and wake up to find yourself in another quite different."

Growing up in Ohio, my two brothers and I would watch the television news with bated breath, hoping to see our school on the list of closures. When that happened, we felt like we had hit the jackpot. My poor mother would help us put on our snow gear; the red wool hats and mittens she knitted, our snow pants, jackets, scarfs, boots with all the buckles, in an area by our back door, called, "the mud room."

Out we would dash to ride our saucer sleds down the hill in our backyard or build igloos inside snow drifts over our next-door neighbor's hillside. Once, we built up the snow so high to make a snow ramp on our hill, that we would go flying up into the air! It's a wonder we didn't kill ourselves, but we survived to remember those exhilarating times.

In Wisconsin, today anyway, my hearty grandkids went to school. They waited for their school bus sitting on top of a huge snow pile by the stop sign on the corner of their street. It is quiet in the house and I'm enjoying the silence. I gaze out the bedroom window at the beautiful snow that lies like a fluffy blanket in the misty air. There is the feeling of being in the middle of a Monet, his *Snow at Argenteuil*, 1875.

So, I get to play "Uncle Buck," for a few days. I'll feed my grandson's fish, Rupert, and do some laundry. Later, I'll dance in the living room with my grandkids when we have our "dance party" after dinner. Right now, the quiet is all the music I need, the quiet on this misty snowy morning when the wind gently brushes the bare branches and swirls the snow around.

How rarely we experience the quiet. Is it because our lives are too busy to notice, or are we afraid to give ourselves this "gift," that life offers us? If we are quiet, what memories will creep into our hearts that will make us sad? Or, what longings will make our hearts ache? But it is in the quiet that we can be thankful for all the people and memories that have made our lives rich, purposeful, and hopefully, mostly happy.

In the quiet of this snowy day, there is the white of the snow, the black of the bare trees, and the gray mist, that gives us "the view," out of this window. As Yoko Ono once said: "Winter passes and one remembers one's perseverance."

46

WHEN SPRING COMES

I was talking to my daughter, Lindsay's mother-in-law, Evonne, the other day. She told me the trumpeter swans have come to rest at her quiet river behind her home in Minnesota. She enjoys the woods nearby, and saw several deer there last November. Soon, she will see new fawns.

"They have chased the Canadian geese away," says Evonne, about the trumpeter swans. "I like the swans better, but their "honk" is very loud! I hope I see some babies this Spring."

In 1933, there were only seventy wild trumpeter swans known to still exist, and they were close to being extinct. But, fortunately, through aerial surveys, several thousand trumpeters were discovered around the Copper River in Alaska.

Through people who cared, the wildlife agencies, there are now over 46,000 trumpeters known to exist today. How fortunate we are, that when some animals are close to extinction, somehow, naturalists or even a small child, can discover that life does go on.

This Spring, I do not want to miss opportunities to rediscover nature. I remember as a small child, the thrill of seeing a robin's nest in the windowsill of our bathroom window one year. When the mother robin was not sitting on her nest, my mom would gently open the window so we could see the beautiful blue eggs. Later, we observed the baby robins, and all too soon we watched the fledglings fly away.

My dear mother would explain to us why the little birds had to eventually leave their nest. We learned valuable lessons in nature. We learned that it is okay to fly, to reach the sky, to live our lives, and how important it was to care for and be mindful of all God's creatures.

Once, in California, my daughter, Ashley, and I found a wounded seagull on the beach. We took him to the wildlife center so he could be rehabilitated. Another time we found a wounded woodpecker we think a cat got hold of. I know that both my daughters learned compassion for all animals through me, as I learned it through my mother's love for all creatures. These gestures might seem small, but they mean so much.

When you go outside this Spring, look, and listen. There is joy all around us in the visual beauty of birds, and in other animals. Where I live, we have hummingbirds. In Wisconsin, where my daughter, Ashley lives, she has visitors, Caroline and Carl, whooping cranes, who sound like a car horn going off.

There is beauty in their songs, even in the honking conversations of whooping cranes and trumpeters, and even more beauty in their presence.

47

GOING TO MY HIGH SCHOOL REUNION

I t has been many years since I went to my last high school reunion. I will not say which one this is, but if I did, you would realize I am over half a century old. Once a year, I return to my hometown of Dayton, Ohio, to see family and friends. I have several friends I keep in touch with and a couple very dear friends from the old neighborhood. I think keeping in touch this way keeps me grounded, somehow. I relish the happy memories of my youth.

In the movie comedy, *Romy and Michelle's High School Reunion*, I think it was Michelle who asked Romy: "What group were we in? Maybe the *B* group. I don't think we were in the *C* group." Romy replies they were in their "own group."

The *A* group was made up of the cheerleaders and jocks. We had our groups, for sure, but it is because we each had our own interests. As an editor of a youth poetry journal, I was in the writers' group. I was also in high school plays, so I guess I was in the actors' group.

I was a "card," in the play, *Alice in Wonderland*. By my senior year in high school, I was the lead sister in the play, *The Egg and I*. I won blue ribbons in contest speech competitions, too. You could also say I was in the softball group. In our senior year, my teammates and I were in first place in our softball league. We did well, despite my losing my contact lens on the field once and stopped the game while everyone helped me look for it. I was on a bowling team. My good friend, Marcia, made the best chocolate chip cookies for our team snack.

I tried out for cheerleading, but got shin splints so that was out. I was not all that coordinated so I did not make the drill team. And, student council, well, was not for me, either. I found my gift of writing poetry when I was sixteen years old and began publishing my poems in *The Cincinnati Enquirer*. Looking back, I think I was in my "own group," too. I did not invent *Post-it Notes*, but I have done all right.

48

HAVE LEGS WILL TRAVEL
(JUNE 2023)

So, after babysitting my granddaughter all day, I start my car to get onto the horrible Los Angeles freeway to head south to my home. I roll down the driver's side window to let in a bit of air while I turn on my air conditioner to my very old car. I start to roll up my window as my car cools down, but the window gets stuck half way up.

Great, I am thinking. Now, I will hear all that traffic noise on my hour-and-a-half drive home. I turn up the volume on my car radio to drown out the traffic noise. Finally, I make it home.

The next day, I take my car once again to my auto repair guy. Lately, I feel like I live at the place. A few weeks prior the cooling pump went out. I dropped my car off. So, I am without my car for a couple of days now. Fortunately, my little town that looks like something out of the movie, *Back to the Future*, is very walkable. I walk a lot into my town and back home. I joined a hiking group and go hiking. But when I thought about walking to my local drugstore to get Father's

Day cards and to the post office to get stamps, I'm thinking to myself: "I can't do *that*! It's too *far*! I'll have to wait until I get my car back from the shop!"

It took me a whole day writing in my home office at my desk until it dawned on me. No, wait a second. People used to do this all the time. I *can* walk to the drugstore and post office. It's not that far. So, I put on my walking shoes and set off. I walked to the drugstore and got some Father's Day cards, then to the post office and got some stamps. Then, I went to our local coffee shop and got some coffee. I sat down at a table outside the coffee shop and wrote some "greetings" to some cool dads, like my two brothers. Then, I walked back to the post office, mailed the cards, and walked home.

And, on my way home, I thought about all the money I was saving on gasoline by walking. In other words, if you have legs and are able to walk, that's a "win-win." No one can charge you $5.50 a gallon for your legs!

49

MOTHER'S DAY IS EVERYDAY

A s devoted moms, we would do anything for our kids. My youngest daughter, Ashley, is doing mountains of laundry right now because her poor daughter caught a stomach bug and well, you know. Years ago, my former mother-in-law told me how she did fourteen loads of laundry because my kids got head lice. I was out of town on a book tour and missed the whole thing!

When it comes to packing kids for trips, Ashley has packing down to a science. My older daughter, Lindsay, is going to discover soon, with her daughter, how many hours of planning it takes with children just to get out the door! I was the "pack-it-up-and-move-it" mom, for our family when we moved from New York to California to Texas. I had to stage our houses and keep them in mint condition to sell them. During the time we were trying to sell our house in New York, this was not easy when you are breastfeeding a baby and trying to keep a toddler from playing "flood the bathroom," and "let's pull every pot out of the cupboard."

In California, when my then husband thought it would be a good idea to move to Texas, I had to entertain potential buyers for three months. When we sold the house, I had to supervise movers with two little kids in tow, as my then husband showed up just at the exact moment the movers were closing the doors on the moving van with all our stuff packed into it.

In Texas, I had to unpack over 400 boxes of stuff and got carpel tunnel in both my wrists, which took a while to recover from. In addition to what I just told you, right now, I'm thinking about all the meals my mom made, all the meals I made for my kids, and all the meals my daughters are making for their kids. It is impossible to comprehend. And, then there were the pets: four dogs, four cats, two rabbits, two ducks, lizards, a chicken, and a fish, that I and my mom, have taken care of.

And, let's not forget birthdays and all the holidays we made "fun," so our kids did, would, and will have wonderful memories of, and hold onto, so traditions will never become a thing of the past. Yes, us moms are "keepers of the flame," the "runny noses," the "heartbreaks" and "triumphs," of lives. So, when you all think of your mothers, just remember where you came from, that labor was like a hundred days of *PMS* rolled into one, but we held it together. Why? Because that first baby cry, that first smile, and all those hugs and kisses is what we live for!

50

SUMMERTIME AND THE LIVING IS...

G oing to the hairdresser is like going to a shrink and spa at the same time, like a "shra-cation." But my hairdresser, Nicole, is a young mom of three kids, loves them to pieces, and is stretched to the max, so she talks to *me*! She does my hair and most of the talking, too. But I am happy to listen.

She worries that her oldest daughter will never find, "Mr. Right." She worries that her youngest daughter will realize mom can't make it to "all" of her softball games and will be devastated. And she worries that her young son, going through the "terrible twos," will be a holy terror forever. As a mom who has juggled swim team practice, dance team practice, drill team practice, soccer practice, cheer leading practice, gymnastics practice, plus all the games and meets, I wish I could tell her that it "all comes out in the wash." Everyone survives, and you are left with many wonderful memories, not the ones where you lived in your car and felt like a member of the "mad-moms-in-minivans," club.

When my "schlep-your-kid" days found me in Plano, Texas, there was a talk show host who would interview these "mad moms" who called into the segments to relay their horror stories. The mom with the craziest story got a prize, like a week's worth of McDonald's hamburgers or something. It was certainly not the gift of a "chauffeur," which would have *really* helped the mom out!

One of the stories went like this: "I couldn't find my pizza I got for the kids and realized it was on top of my van as I drove away!" My worst story was when we had just moved from New York to northern California in July, 1986. My kids were six months and three years old at the time. We moved across the country with one dog, two cars and enough stuff to fill up a football stadium. I was still trying to recover from giving birth and managing my new role as a "zombie."

So, I took my kids to Toys "R" Us, and we did some shopping. After I put my kids into the car, and the toys we bought into the car, I headed for home. I was half way there when I realized I had forgotten something. In a panic, I raced back to the exact spot where I had parked the car at Toys "R" Us to find what I had left behind. But my brand new double-seated stroller was nowhere to be found!

I was shocked, then mad at myself for doing such a dumb thing. Then, I was relieved that it was the stroller and not one of my kids I had forgotten. Maybe I'm not such a bad mommy after all, I reasoned. Through all the craziness, I realized one thing, how "hyper-vigilant" I was about not losing my kids and making sure they had the "hap-hap-happiest" growing up period that I could possibly manage.

Why? Not because I was a mad-mom-in-a-minivan. It was and is because they are my "heart." When my oldest daughter, Lindsay, gave birth to her first child not long ago, she realized something that for us moms, is not always easy to explain. About her newborn daughter she said: "It's crazy how all of a sudden your heart is outside your body and I would do anything for her!" I rest my case.

PART IV

THE PEOPLE WE MEET; THE FRIENDS WE MAKE

51

MY FRIEND, ERMA BOMBECK

When I was sixteen years old, God gave me the gift of writing. He has always been my inspiration, and so has my friend and famous humorist, Erma Bombeck. I began submitting my poems to such publications as *The Cincinnati Enquirer*. Readers loved them so much that a reporter came to my house to interview me and take my picture. It was then I thought to write a letter to Erma, asking for her advice. At the time, she was writing a column for *The Kettering-Oakwood Times*, in my hometown of Dayton, Ohio.

Erma touched the lives of so many housewives in the 1960's. She was syndicated in over 900 newspapers and read by over 30 million people. She even wrote several books, such as, *Family – The Ties That Bind...and Gag!* Erma knew that raising kids, husbands, all kinds of pets (barking, creeping, crawling), was not an easy task for any mother. And the mothers loved her. Erma understood the trials of a toilet that overflowed, a child's inconsolable tears, and sleepless nights from monsters under the bed.

One day, a letter arrived for me. It was from Erma. Thrilled beyond belief, I carefully opened it. She wrote: *Anne, you are on your way at sixteen. When I was your age, I couldn't write my name on my gym suit! Good luck and God bless. Erma Bombeck.* It was at that moment I knew I was on my way as a writer. Years later, when I published my first book, I sent her a copy, thanking her again. She wrote me back this letter: *While I'd like to take the credit, it was all you! Congratulations! God bless, Erma.*

52

MR. JOHN KUEHN

We were seniors at Fairmont West High School in the autumn of 1971 when Mr. Kuehn came to teach our English class. He was young, only twenty-three years old, I believe. Bucking the system a little bit, he had us put our desks in a circle, so we could better communicate with one another. I thought that was brilliant and wonderful. He was soft-spoken but had a commanding voice. And he smiled more than most teachers. I think many of us wanted to learn from him. He got us to think about life, believe in our dreams, and believe that we could achieve them.

Being a budding writer, I liked him even more when he encouraged me to be an editor for our junior poetry magazine. At a time when I felt my parents did not understand or support me, Mr. Kuehn did, and I will be forever grateful.

Mr. Kuehn encouraged me when I wanted to attend Ohio University, not because it had the reputation as a "party school," but because there were many well-known professional writers who were professors there. I wanted to learn from them. As serious as I was in my desire to be a writer and already publishing my poems in magazines and newspapers, my parents, I felt, still did not understand my dreams, but Mr. Kuehn did.

Years later, when I returned to his classroom after my first book was published to introduce my two young daughters to him, Mr. Kuehn was very welcoming. I did not want to interrupt his classroom full of students, but he encouraged us to come in and introduced me to his class. Then, he revealed something that I knew nothing about. He totally surprised me and made me feel so good about myself. In front of my kids and everyone he said: "Do you know that I've used your senior thesis on e. e. cummings as my model thesis for the past twenty-five years?" I wanted to cry, because you see, I had just published my first book. It was excerpted in three editions of *Reader's Digest*. I had just appeared on the *Today Show*, but my father, from whom I desperately wanted approval, had little to say. So, thank you Mr. Kuehn, for making a difference in my life, as teachers who really care, can do.

53

PETE SEEGER, DANIEL KEYES AND WALTER TEVIS

My life at college from 1972 to 1976 was indeed an eye opener. I discovered why Ohio University had a reputation as a party school. In Crook Hall on the West Green my dorm room was in a hallway with several sophomore girls, physical education majors, who loved to party. It was not coed, but we had male visitors who thought it was fun to pull the fire alarms and watch the girls come outside into the courtyard in their curlers and pajamas. I spent a lot of time in quiet solitude in this beautiful campus beneath the big oak trees or by the river, reading books of poetry by such poets as Pablo Neruda, Octavio Paz, James Tate, Keats, Lawrence Ferlinghetti, and W.S Merwin. I was in a world of my own and loved it.

The hills were gorgeous in autumn, my most favorite season. I had obtained several independent studies to write poems. One professor, Dr. Nico Suarez, encouraged me to submit a couple poems to Pete Seeger's anthology, *From the Hudson to the world: Voices of the river*, to protest the pollution of the Hudson River. Edited by Charles Hayes, it was published by Hudson River Sloop Clearwater in 1978. Two of my poems were published in this anthology and another poem in *Mademoiselle*.

The 1970's were a time of much unrest. The Vietnam War was raging, as were many protests and riots across our country. On "Little Sibs" weekend, my brothers who came to visit me, experienced a riot that broke out after a James Taylor concert at the Convocation Center.

We quickly got out of there and ran up the hill into Little Caesars, thinking things would die down by the time we ordered our pizza. It did not. We turned a table on its side and hid behind it in the back of the restaurant. We watched out of the big picture window as policemen were tear gassing students running all over the place as they tried to control the crowds. We were stuck there until 3:00 a.m. I would later write in my screenplay, *The Peacemaker*, about the 1965 Watts Riots, regarding my character, Barbara, a waitress: "alarmed, she gazes out the big picture window at people rioting and the Army National Guard barreling down the street..."

During my junior year, I met coal miners and their families in Appalachia, when I interviewed them for an article I wrote on black lung disease. It was for the *Mademoiselle* Guest Editor competition and I won honorable mention. In my senior year, I became editor of our literary journal, *Sphere*. I had the pleasure of making friends with authors Daniel Keyes (*Flowers For Algenon*) and Walter Tevis (*The Queen's Gambit*), who agreed to be my judges for a poetry and short story contest I held. Looking back. I surprise myself, at the risks I took in meeting these amazing people and making new friends. As for Pete Seeger, I did finally meet him as a young mother and new author, living in San Rafael, California. Pete was on a book tour and was at our local bookstore. I showed him the anthology he published my poems in, years ago. He smiled and signed one of the pages my poem was published on, and we had a chance to talk. How I loved his songs: "Where Have All the Flowers Gone?" "If I Had a Hammer," "Turn, Turn, Turn." They were like sunshine in summer, a soft breeze blowing through the window in the midst of swirling storms in our young lives.

54

SWEDEN, ENGLAND, BARB, AND GILLIAN
(SUMMER 1975)

I don't know who was braver, but I think it was my mother. She convinced my father to let me be part of a study abroad program for the summer at Trinity College, Oxford University, England, after my junior year at Ohio University. There was one other girl, Debra, from my college, who was part of this tutorial group. We joined other students from the University of Massachusetts. I flew alone from Dayton, Ohio, to Boston's Logan airport where I met up with Debra. We then connected with the other students, and from there, our group flew to London.

We had some time to travel before classes began at Trinity College, so I went to visit my cousin, Barb, and her then husband, Bo, in Gothenburg, Sweden. Upon my arrival, we traveled to their summer home in Ramsvik. The sunrise in my cozy attic bedroom woke me up at 3:00 a.m., which was quite a surprise, but I loved how the sun never quite set during the summer.

We sailed to various islands in their sailboat, *Frida*, and ate shrimp from the porch at their home, as we watched the purple and orange sky and the sun not quite set at 10:00 at night. I remember the air smelling so fresh, and seeing colorful flowers everywhere, and blonde-haired children playing on the beach.

At Trinity College, I was in awe at living in the middle of history. My room was up Staircase 13, and I had a view of the beautiful President's Garden. My bedroom and sitting room were something out of *Harry Potter*, as was our dining hall, where young boys dressed in navy suit jackets and tan trousers, would come up to us and ask: "white or black?" They were asking if we wanted our coffee black or with cream, to go with our scrambled eggs smothered in stewed tomatoes.

Our classes consisted of studies in art and Shakespeare, and one of my dearest friends I made while there was a young artist, Gillian, who had long strawberry blonde hair, blue eyes, and freckles, and looked not too unlike, "Pippi Longstocking." Her mother was British, and her father was an American English professor at University of Massachusetts, on sabbatical to write a book on the poet, Lord Byron. Gillian had been to England many times, having stayed with her grandmother, who had a home in Abingdon-on-the-Thames (Abingdon).

She made my summer so exciting, as on our weekends, we often took the train to London. We stayed in youth hostels, and toured museums, like the Victoria and Albert Museum, visited castles, like Kensington Palace, and ate in many wonderful eateries like Ye Olde Cheshire Cheese Pub. I remember they had a garden on the rooftop, and served us fresh strawberries from that garden. Gillian knew London like the "back of her hand," so I felt blessed to have such an amazing travel companion and friend.

After our daily studies at Oxford University, we often went to a quaint tea room and had tea and scones in the afternoon. And, once, we took the train to visit her grandmother in Abingdon. It was also lovely seeing plays, like *Cymbeline*, in Stratford-upon-Avon, Shakespeare's birthplace. And we paid homage to novelist George Orwell's grave site in Oxfordshire.

Back in the states, we went our separate ways into separate lives, but kept in touch. My friend, Gillian, later married a nice lawyer named, Jim, and they had two daughters. They settled in Amherst, Massachusetts, where my grandfather, Dr. George L. Cutton, my mother's father, attended Amherst College, many years ago. I took my daughters to visit Gillian one autumn when they were ten and twelve. Gillian, by this time, had been painting and displayed many of her paintings in local galleries. She gave us two of her paintings, one for each of my daughters. They ended up in my home, for which I am glad.

It has been years since we have seen one another, but Gillian will always be that light in my life, the friend who made a difference, the friend who makes me feel young again, whenever I think of her.

55

NEW YORK CITY, HARPER'S BAZAAR, JERRY HALL, AND LATER, FRITZ FRELENG

I met my first husband, David, in college and we married after his second year in law school, August of 1976. When he graduated, as promised, we moved from our small apartment in Little Italy in Cleveland, Ohio, to New York City, Manhattan, the upper East Side, specifically. We had our plan all figured out, as we loaded up our *U-Hall* truck in May 1977, and headed east. My parents came to visit and help us move our stuff into the truck. I did not really understand my mother's breaking heart at the time when her parting words to me were: "You'll go to New York and you'll change!" It was a deep cut that hurt for a long time. I wanted her to be encouraging and happy for me. I was going to fulfill my dream of being a writer in New York City.

Driving along the Pennsylvania Turnpike seemed like a dream come true. We were embarking on our first adventure. My then husband had acquired a job with a prestigious law firm. I was armed with my portfolio of published work. We were on our way! Then, as we pulled up to the toll booth, we realized our truck was out of gas. A faulty gas cap was the culprit. A *U-Haul* representative came to our rescue and fixed the gas cap problem, and we were on our way again.

As we rolled into Manhattan, we realized that trucks were not allowed on Third Avenue, so we had to do a detour right through Harlem. Finally, we made it to Second Avenue and our four-story apartment building on East 81st Street. As we began to unload the truck, having to double park like most people, a fire truck came screaming around the corner. My then husband directed him to go around us, but the fire fighter waved his finger at him and told him to, "Move it!" As David jumped into our *U-Hall* truck, doors still open, he sped away to go around the block. Our television set took a nose dive off the filing cabinet and that was our "welcome to the Big Apple!"

Two months later, the New York City blackout hit on July 13-14. Brave strangers helped direct traffic because the traffic lights were out; many people in high rises had no water because the water pumps didn't work. The night of the blackout, some young woman in our building got stuck in the elevator. David and some other guys managed to get her out. Another young woman, Pam, down the hall, invited several of us residents into her apartment lit by candles, for cake. As several of us sat on the floor, we listened to the news on her small transistor radio. We talked and comforted one another, and that is how we met our neighbors!

Two evenings later, I was gazing out of our apartment window at our dark silent city, and talking to my mother on the telephone. Suddenly, all the lights in the New York City began lighting up the sky one by one! I will never forget that feeling of exhilaration! It was like Christmas!

During my time in Manhattan, I initially worked as an assistant editor for an employee magazine for Morgan Guaranty Trust Company on Wall Street. Always wanting to work for a woman's magazine, I later became senior associate editor at *Lady's Circle* located in a Brownstone on 28th near Broadway. I think it was the most fun I ever had on a job, laughing and working with my editor, Susan, and two staff members, Fran and Mary. Mr. Adrian Lopez, our publisher, gave us a lot of freedom to attend many press events as long as we got our work done. Covering a book talk by Phil Donahue at Tavern on the Green, a jewelry fashion show on a yacht, and a party at the opening of Studio 54, are some of my most exciting memories.

A few years later, I joined the staff at *Harper's Bazaar* as an assistant features editor. At *Harper's Bazaar*, just like in the movie, *The Devil Wears Prada*, I was the Andrea "Andy" Sachs working with our managing editor, who will remain anonymous. But I will say her interesting remarks on one writer's article prompted him to threaten to sue the magazine. Fortunately, the remarks were in pencil and she made me erase all of them!

Our editor-in-chief was a tough but mostly nice man, whose wife floated from department to department telling everyone what to do when she got bored. Occasionally, Jerry Hall, Mick Jagger's ex, would breeze through the fashion department to discuss business with the fashion editor, while the fashion assistants fought like cats and dogs over the latest sample shoes sent from Milan.

I had amazing opportunities to write articles for all these publications, but at the same time, I was determined to build my freelance business and get my articles published in every woman's magazine around. I was being published in *McCall's, Working Mother, Ladies' Home Journal, Mademoiselle, Seventeen, Redbook, Bride's, Reader's Digest,* and others. By the time we moved into our first home in Mt. Kisco, an hour north of the city, I was one of several authors writing chapters for a fifty-year celebration book of *Bride's.* The highlight for me was working with the founder's granddaughter, and looking at wedding announcements through the years in a special room in Tiffany & Co.

Since there was a delay with the editors of *The Bride,* I still was writing the honeymoon chapter going into labor to have my first child, Lindsay. Thank goodness my mom was there to help me, so I could finish my chapter right after giving birth.

I was on a roll as a full-time freelancer when my second daughter, Ashley, was born. I was a member of the American Society of Journalists and Authors (ASJA), and a frequent moderator at our annual workshops. But my then husband announces that his company is moving us to San Francisco. In those days, the way to do business was through lunches or dinners with editors, as we did not have the internet or zoom. I was crushed.

But God would not let me give up on my dreams. A couple years later, I wrote a book, was on the *Today Show,* and met Friz Freleng, the creator of *Bugs Bunny,* in the Green Room. It was such an honor to meet him. When it was my turn to be interviewed by Katie Couric, I love to say that *Bugs Bunny* (the new voice, Jeff Bergman) introduced me.

56

SAN RAFAEL, CARLOS SANTANA, ROBIN WILLIAMS, AND ANN CURTIS

"It feels like people are moving in slow motion out here!" I said to my girlfriend, Roberta, who was my neighbor in our suburb of Mt. Kisco, north of New York City. I missed my friends back home, but as a family we all soon grew to love the San Francisco Bay Area where we lived in San Rafael, from July 1986 to December 1994. The movie, *American Graffiti*, was filmed in part on Fourth Street.

We soon adjusted to the pace of living in the west. I learned that one of our neighbors in our area was Carlos Santana and his then wife, Debbie. When city officials wanted to cut out our arts and music program at our kids' elementary school, they stepped in and donated money to keep it going. Carlos became all us moms' "calm friend." Whenever we all felt frazzled picking up our kids after school, Carlos was so chill. He helped all of us moms feel better chatting with us.

My oldest daughter, Lindsay, was in the same kindergarten class as Carlos' son, Salvador. During "career day,"

Carlos came and played his guitar for the kids. I volunteered a lot in Lindsay's classroom, and I still remember Carlos sitting in a small chair, guitar in hand, playing and singing.

During those early days, Taco Bell was often my "go-to," as a mom running all over the place to get my two daughters to ballet, gymnastics, and swim practice. One day, around dinnertime, Lindsay and I stopped into Taco Bell, and who should be there picking up a bunch of tacos but Robin Williams! We were a bit surprised to see "Mrs. Doubtfire," but Robin seemed so friendly. I said hello when he looked in our direction and he smiled at us. Oh, how I wanted to go over and talk with him, but I didn't. I only wish, looking back, that we could have enjoyed a conversation together while we waited for our tacos.

"Mom, can I join the swim team?" my daughter, Lindsay, asked me, when she was eight years old. She joined the Marlins swim team, and I later got her sister, Ashley, involved at age six, so I could be at one place at one time. Ashley was a dynamo with the butterfly stroke, and Lindsay excelled at freestyle.

Later, when they joined a different swim team, their coach was none-other-than, Ann Curtis, an Olympic gold medal winner in the 1948 Summer Olympics in Great Britain for her 400-meter freestyle. I had the privilege of interviewing Ann for an article I wrote for the *Marin Independent Journal*. Lindsay and Ann's photo was also published in the newspaper, as Ann was coaching my daughter on some freestyle strokes. She was a gracious lady and I am so thankful to have met her.

57

TEXAS, MRS. BREEZE, MRS. MOUSTROM, ZIG ZIGLAR, JEB STUART, MARY KAY, AND OTHER FINE PEOPLE

Leaving beautiful California for the plains of Plano, Texas, was not an easy move in December of 1994. My then husband, David, decided his brother had better ideas and convinced him of greater job opportunities in Dallas. My daughters were older and it was hard on them to say goodbye to their friends. My youngest daughter, Ashley, was especially fond of Mrs. Breeze, her third-grade teacher, and was very sad to leave her class. She barely had a chance to say goodbye. Mrs. Breeze really did have the face and sweet personality of an angel. On our first Valentine's Day in our new home, we received a package addressed to my daughter. It was filled with Valentines from all the students in Mrs. Breeze's class, including one from Mrs. Breeze herself. That really made my daughter's day.

And, my older daughter, Lindsay's kindergarten teacher, Mrs. Moustrom, somehow, kept track of each student in every one of her classes. Years later, when Lindsay graduated from high school she received a letter of congratulations from Mrs. Moustrom.

It was not easy to make friends with people in Texas. I do not know why, but the mothers seemed to be more interested in gossip and how to move their kids ahead in sports and various activities. Schools in this area seemed to put a lot of pressure on the kids to succeed. I remember Ashley coming home in tears after she got off the school bus in those early days, because she was assigned more homework than she had received from her teachers in California. Years later, when Ashley was settled as a freshman in a competitive college back in Southern California, I asked her: "Which is harder Ashley, high school or college?" She replied: "High school, Mom."

But my kids made new friends and I joined a Bunko group among the nice neighbor ladies on my street. Betsy and I were especially close as "warriors" in our battle of the "moms against the construction workers" on our new homes, who were more than willing to blame us or question our intelligence regarding their "negligence" in making things "right."

When Betsy and her husband went out to dinner one night, leaving her two daughters, Pamela, eleven, and Christy, nine, to wait for the pizza guy, who would have ever thought the "worst thing," could happen. When the doorbell rang, and Pamela and Christy answered the door, they took their pizza from the delivery guy. No problems. But the minute they stepped away from the door and were in the kitchen, their chandelier in the foyer crashed to the floor! "Don't worry," I told Betsy. "It's not real; it's all in our imaginations." At least that's what the construction workers wanted us to think!

When I joined Prestonwood Baptist Church, I never in a million years thought I would have Zig Ziglar as my encouragers class teacher, and boy, did he encourage us! I never met anyone more enthusiastic about life than Zig. He always kept us laughing. "People often say that motivation doesn't last. Well, neither does bathing – that's why we recommend it daily!" Zig would say. Or, "the more grateful you are for what you have the more you will have to be grateful for!" Or, "duty makes us do things well, but love makes us do them beautifully."

As a writer, it still became a bit of a struggle to find my place in the world. My old writing group, The American Society of Journalists and Authors, Inc., did not have a chapter in Dallas, but one day, I noticed a tiny advertisement in *The Dallas Morning News*. It was an ad for the Dallas Screenwriters Association. I decided to join and fell in love with reading screenplays, learning about screenplays from various amazing speakers we had once a month, and writing screenplays. I even won an award from a *Writer's Digest* screenwriting contest in 2003 for one of my scripts. We heard from filmmaker and actor, Shane Black (*Lethal Weapon* franchise, *The Long Kiss Goodnight*); screenwriter Jeb Stuart (*The Fugitive*), and a woman who became a good friend of mine, Stephanie Moore, then Director of admissions for special programs in the UCLA Professional Screenwriters Program.

When I attended the Austin Film Festival one year, I enjoyed the rare privilege of having coffee and a two-hour conversation with Jeb Stuart, who was next door neighbors at the time with Henry, the brother of a good friend of mine, Howland.

While I'm not sure this was a "divine appointment," I do believe God put the dream of writing screenplays into my heart, too.

In the late 1990's, as I was on the verge of obtaining a possible new book deal, my then husband barked: "Why don't you get a *real* job!" I was fortunate to get a job with Mary Kay, Inc., as a senior instructional designer, and put together audio tapes and booklets for the thousands of Mary Kay beauty consultants. I felt sorry for many of them, who were not adept at marketing and had loads of debt. There must be something I can do, I wondered, and God gave me the answer. I gathered six of our top earning Mary Kay Directors and met with them. They all had been in debt at one time, got out of debt and became very successful.

I met with them at a restaurant one day and we talked. I asked them all kinds of questions about how they got into debt, how they got out, how did they become so successful. Later, with the permission of my boss, who became heavily involved, I helped produce a video that was later shown to over 3,000 beauty consultants at their national convention in Dallas, Texas. They loved the video so much that many of them were in tears at finally getting some answers and help. My boss took all the credit for this highly successful video, but I still felt good that I had helped so many beauty consultants.

It was while I worked at Mary Kay, Inc., that we employees had the opportunity to celebrate Mary Kay's last birthday on earth with her. What a privilege it was to see her blow out the candles on her huge pink birthday cake and listen to the Mary Kay choir sing her favorites hymns. She was a gracious lady, always encouraging us with affirmations and advice: "God gave us two ears and one mouth for a reason!" she would say.

And, later, when I was writing articles for *The Dallas Morning News*, I had a wonderful health and lifestyles section editor, Patricia. I met some fascinating people I wrote articles about, like Hoa, a Vovinam master, who helped our Green Berets fight the communists in the jungles of Vietnam during the Vietnam War.

58

HERMOSA BEACH, UCLA, STEPHANIE MOORE, AND MICHAEL

(2006 TO 2016)

Both of my daughters ended up at the same college in Southern California. I was very happy they were together for one year, when Lindsay was a senior, and Ashley was a freshman. I was happy that they had decided they wanted to be back on the West Coast. Their father did not want them to go to college in Texas, and since his mother lived in San Diego, he considered it a right choice. I think God might have had something to do with that, when He opened the door for me to also move out to California in June 2006.

I drove out to the West Coast in my silver PT Cruiser, with three cats, Tyson, Hannah and Lucy, and my dog, Charley. A girlfriend came with me, as she wanted to see her daughter in Fresno. I was very glad to have the help and company. I figured out hotels that allowed pets, and for two nights, all of us slept in the same room. I almost had a heart attack, though, when I could not find Lucy. My girlfriend and I tore the room apart looking for her. We could not figure out where she could have gone because we never opened the door once we had all pets inside our hotel room. Finally, we thought to look up inside the recliner and there she was, hiding.

It was quite the drive through some gorgeous landscapes across America. When we exited off the freeway at Artesia for Hermosa Beach, I'll never forget coming up over the hill on Manhattan Beach Blvd. and seeing the very blue Pacific Ocean. It was breathtaking! I thanked God for bringing me to this peaceful place where I figured I could restore my broken heart. No one anticipates going into a marriage for it to end, or to break up a family, but some things a marriage can't seem to survive. I learned that people change only if they want to change, and that I had choices, too. Call me crazy, but I believe it was God's choice for me most of all. As humans, we can choose to remember the good times of our past, appreciate the lessons, and embrace the path God has for us.

Through my friend, Stephanie Moore, Director of Admissions of special programs at UCLA at the time, and my collection of viable screenplays, I was able to go to college, too. I was accepted into UCLA's Professional Screenwriting Program, and before all the politics, it was an incredible place to be. I hope it will be like I remember it again in the future. So, I was a student. I felt young, and believed that God had truly blessed me with a chance to be wholly free for the first time in my life.

As I got settled into my apartment with a tiny view of the ocean from my kitchen window, I began taking Charley and myself for long walks along the shore. The waves were a balm to my soul. I loved watching the white caps toss their spray up into the air like wild horses and enfold into deep blue curls. I loved watching the sun's rays sparkle on the water like a million diamonds, and the locals walking their dogs on The Strand.

I slept on a blow-up mattress for almost a month, grieving losses and feeling a bit paralyzed. But, little by little, I was determined to keep moving forward. I figured it was time to buy some furniture. Having so many decisions made for me in my lifetime, it was scary at first to buy my own furniture, the styles I wanted. I was like a kid in a candy store, and felt so proud of myself when my apartment was fully decorated, and it looked amazing.

I was a student! I was living in California as a single woman. I had a job working as a reader of screenplays at Gold Circle Films, joined the Hollywood Prayer Network, and made several nice friends. I attended many great workshops, where I met such amazing people as actor Martin Landau, director Mark Rydell and screenwriter, Lyle Kessler. Though terribly lonely at times, I was enjoying my single life. The thought of dating never really crossed my mind until my oldest daughter one day said: "Mom, you should meet someone!"

Whether it was good timing or if I should have allowed myself more time to be single, wisdom either eludes us, or the longing for love takes over, I guess. It was here, in Hermosa Beach, less than a year later, that I met Michael, who would become my second husband. He was tall, dark, and handsome, and could almost be a double for the actor, Sean Connery, "007." Who could resist?

On our first date we had coffee at a little cafe near Hermosa Beach Pier, walked under an umbrella as it started to drizzle that April 24th day. We enjoyed each other's company so much we had dinner at an Italian restaurant, then coffee at our café again. When it really started pouring rain, we ducked into my car and talked until 10:00 that evening, with rain enveloping us.

Our favorite song became "Bless The Broken Road," by Rascal Flatts. Michael's former wife had died and left three sons behind. It was a lot to take on, perhaps, but we figured God could mend two broken hearts in love. We were married six weeks later, barefoot, on Butterfly Beach, in Santa Barbara, on June 7, 2007. It was by the ocean where we had our best memories over nine years, full of fun and laughter. And, it was the last place I took my once strong husband to see, before he went to Heaven, after a long battle with ALS, on September 18, 2016.

59

MY FRIEND, HEIDI (1992). THEY OUGHT TO GIVE A NOBEL PEACE PRIZE TO CORPORATE WIVES

I have a former neighbor, Heidi, who moved fifteen times due to her husband's jobs in the corporate world. Her daughter had been in fifteen different schools. "It's okay, though," says the zombie-eyed cheerful mother. "My daughter has always adapted well, because I've taught her to look at moving like an adventure." That's nice, I thought, as I looked at my friend and figured she could use a big hug and prayers. I could not believe she was still alive to tell the tale!

One story Heidi told me was that they had only forty-eight hours to move out of the country of Guatemala because things were getting dicey. Of course, they knew that. Their daughter almost got kidnapped for ransom. Heidi was not about to wait for her clothes to dry, or the souffle to fall from the vibrations of random bullets in their backyard. "Forget your belongings!" they were told. "We'll ship everything to you after you are back in the states!"

One year, Heidi, with three children under five years old,

had to move to Juneau, Alaska, in January, by herself. Her husband had already arrived, working his new job, and was looking for a house. "There I was, getting off the plane. It was 2:00 in the afternoon, pitch black outside, and the wind almost blew me over with my baby in my arms!" she told me.

Heidi made the best of the situation. She learned to ski, made friends, learned to speak Russian, and wound up being the weather anchor at a local television station. But, after two years of driving on black ice, fighting bears over the barbecued burgers on her patio grill, and almost losing her son in a muddy swamp, she was ready to move back home to California.

But her corporate moving days were not quite over. She had to move to Silicon Valley, where her Alaskan Huskie, not used to closed in spaces, knocked her husband's boss's wife flat on her back at the front door when she arrived, unannounced, to welcome Heidi to the neighborhood! Of course, this did not help Heidi to move back to the city she really wanted to be in, San Rafael. The boss liked her husband and decided to keep him with the Silicon Valley company.

What eventually did it for Heidi was her *foot*! She put it *down*! When her beloved grandmother died and left her the house that Heidi practically grew up in, she saw this event as her big chance. You'd have to be an idiot to sell a house with the breathtaking 360-degree view of San Francisco Bay, and Heidi was far from it. She had a plan. First, she had these tall bushes cleared away to make room for the gorgeous view. She cleaned the house, had repairs and updates done, and voilà, she was home to stay. She enrolled her three kids in the nearby school, and planted herself like some Wisteria vine. And just to add that "extra" touch, she christened it with her new baby! Her husband found a new job just ten minutes away! Now, if she doesn't deserve the Nobel Peace Prize, I don't know who does!

60

MY FRIEND, RHEA

Over fifty-two years ago, a young mother of two sons, Rhea Zakich, lost her voice when she was stricken by a throat ailment. She endured two operations to remove growths on her vocal cords and was told she could not speak for at least three months. In fact, the doctor told her: "I don't know if you will ever speak again." Unable to talk to anyone, especially her family, after receiving notoriety for her amazing work with the mothers and children in the ghetto after the 1965 Watts Riots, she fell into a deep despair.

When she tried to write notes to her sons, Darin, age ten, and Dean, age nine, they just threw them into the trash. And, her husband, Dan, patted her on the shoulder and went off to work. When she went to a party, her friends talked about her as if she was not there. Her life could not have been worse.

But one day her son, Darin, came home crying and poured his heart out to her about a bully at school. Her other son, Dean, wanted to talk about being afraid. A few days later, a neighbor girl who had gotten pregnant and feared her father would throw her out of the house, was sobbing on Rhea's kitchen table.

Rhea just listened. She prayed to God in her head and heart for answers: "Oh, God, how can I communicate with family and friends around me? How can I tell people about You without a voice? How can I serve You?" God gave Rhea an answer.

While her sons were at school, she gathered paper, pencils, glue, and created a game about communication, sharing your feelings, where there were no winners or losers. The winning part was in one's ability to share feelings in answering a question on a card they picked, while other game players had to be quiet until they landed on a "comment" spot.

Working hard to put together several game boards, she was happy with herself. As the glue on the game boards was drying on her kitchen table, she turned out the light and went to bed. The next morning, all the game boards were curled up like potato chips. Heartbroken, Rhea threw everything into the trash. But a couple of days later, just before the garbage collectors arrived, a small boy dug one of the gameboards, dice and game markers out of the trash can and brought everything home to his mother.

This mother was thrilled that her son wanted to play this game, because you see, he had just lost his father and was not speaking at all. Together, the mother and son salvaged this game and played it. The boy shared his feelings of losing his father and began talking again. Several weeks later, a neighbor and his wife mortgaged their home to help Rhea manufacture her game. She sold it to a company, Talicor, in 1973, and the rest, is history.

To date, millions of games of the The *Ungame* have been sold all over the world, since Rhea created her game over fifty years ago! She also got her voice back. In fact, Rhea has given speeches and prayer workshops all over the world. Families, couples, children, other people are better able to communicate with each other and have restored relationships. It has even helped sex trafficked girls in Thailand to heal from trauma, after being rescued.

Rhea and I have been good friends for over thirty years. As a journalist, I wrote an article about her. I had discovered *The Ungame* and played it with my daughters, when they were children. I later wrote a screenplay, *The Peacemaker*, about her incredible work with the mothers and children in Watts at a time when the area was still smoldering from one of the worst riots in history, in 1965.

So, we had lunch together the other day. I loved visiting with her, as always, but felt badly because my screenplay about her life has not yet been produced, though I have tried. She looked at me and said: "It's okay. Maybe it's time to let it go." My heart was breaking because she is not going to be with us much longer and I so desperately want the world to know about her. But she looked at me again and said: "Let God."

61

MY NEIGHBOR, FAYE
(HERMOSA BEACH, 2006-2007)

After months of making excuses that I am too busy, I finally went to visit Faye. She was my neighbor during the year I lived at Hermosa Beach. Faye was in her mid-80's when we met. She was a white-haired, blue-eyed spunky gal who drove a blue 1959 Buick Electra. She lived in one of the last remaining cottages built in Hermosa Beach, yellow with brown trim, a big front porch with a swing, patio in the back with a grand view of the ocean.

I bring Faye tea bags. She puts the kettle on the stove to boil water. We sit at a wooden table on benches in her cozy yellow kitchen that is 1950's modern. Her whole house makes me feel like I have gone back in time. An old white rotary telephone sits on the Formica kitchen countertop next to the cookie jar. A warm breeze blows the lace curtains that frame the windows looking out to the ocean. The kettle sings and Faye picks it up by the black handle. She pours the boiling water over the tea bags in their white cups. Time stops.

We talk about our troubles. Faye tells me the story of how she fractured her wrist last autumn. "It was the craziest thing!" she begins. "I felt so stupid. I was dancing, and part of my skirt got caught up in the air conditioner vent and pulled me down to the floor! I sat there, stunned, until a friend helped me up."

Faye is quite the dancer. She does the jitterbug, the fox trot, and so many other dances at this local seniors' center. I knew, when I heard her story, that her ego was fractured, too, that day. We all want to feel like we can be good at something no matter how old we are, without air conditioners getting in our way. We want to know that maybe we can last a little bit longer, dance the dance with pizzazz, and go out with a bang!

I like to think that's how Faye, my dear friend, left this world, not like being shot out of a canon, but flying, in the blink of an eye, into the arms of Jesus.

62

MY HANDYMAN IS A TREASURE

I got my house painted a while ago and needed some new hardware for my doors. I went to my local hardware store and the sales clerks were very helpful. They all wore cute aprons and were "Johnny-on-the-Spot" ready to help me, like the "pit crew" at a car race track.

Several days later, when I picked up my door handles they had ordered for me, I asked for a recommendation for a handyman. They gave me his card. I was thrilled and secretly prayed he would show up. Not only did Malcolm show up on time, but he even brought his cute little dog, "Rocket," who could have been the body double for Toto, in the movie, *Wizard of Oz*.

Malcolm worked diligently putting new handles on my doors. He even fixed my backdoor to be more secure. And, he followed up afterwards by text to make sure I was happy with his job. Later, I had him fix the metal overhang on the backdoor to my garage and the sagging ceiling in there. He even put in a brighter light over my washing machine and dryer. I was so pleased with him that I could not stop bragging about Malcolm's work to my girlfriends.

Now, Robin and Grace have hired him and are equally happy. Robin grabbed him right away before recommending him to Nancy, who, once she gets a good handyman never lets him go. Now, if I need something fixed around my house I might have to hire another handyman, but I got Malcolm first, and he appreciates the business, so I have not lost him forever.

To us, he is like an angel, a real godsend. We have no idea where he came from except, Ireland, years ago. But, next time, I might just have to keep my best kept secret, a secret.

63

EVERYONE SHOULD KNOW A MRS. MUGGS

(SPRING, 2023)

Whether she is an Amelia Bedelia, a Pippi Longstocking, or Annie Oakley, I believe I met them all in a lady I'll call, Mrs. Muggs. This is not her real name, but this delightful widow lady from Texas graced my town not long ago through my good friend, Judy.

Mrs. Muggs is an artist, but not just any artist. She paints her beautiful floral creations on tea cups and plates. She wanted to tour the antique shops in my little town, as she was here to teach master art classes, of which my friend was a student. The three of us had lunch, first, at a cute restaurant in an historic house. Flowers hugged the walkways as we entered. While Judy and I wore simple tops and jeans, Mrs. Muggs was dressed as something out of the movie, *Pollyanna*. At least, this is how I will always remember her, as Polly Harrington, Pollyanna's aunt, played by Jane Wyman. Halley Mills played Pollyanna. The film was based on the 1913 novel, *Pollyanna*, by Eleanor H. Porter.

As Judy and I sat at a table in this lovely restaurant with Mrs. Muggs, in her elegant dress of pastel colors and flowery straw hat, I felt transported back in time to a most peaceful era. So, it was quite interesting when Mrs. Muggs began talking about life on her ranch in San Antonio with her goats, and how she almost shot a guest with her rifle in the middle of the night who had mistaken her bedroom for his. She did not go into any more detail, but I sensed she was a tough old bird that nobody better mess with.

I feel blessed to have known a few Mrs. Muggs characters in my lifetime. When I was five years old, there was a lady down the street who had fifty cats. How my mom allowed me to walk to her house to go see her cats by myself I'll never know. But life was much safer in the 1950's.

Then, there was the lady next door to our first house, Evelyn. She made the best cornbread and sometimes invited me over for dinner because I was friends with her son, Michael. We were six years old. And, there was another lady, Mrs. Lamworth, a widow, who had a beautiful vegetable garden across the country road where my Aunt Margie lived in Palatine, Illinois. My two boy cousins, Doug and Larry, loved to taunt her when they were bored and say things like: "Hey old lady; you're hoeing all wrong!" When my aunt made them apologize, they realized that she was nice, when she gave them tomatoes from her garden. That was the summer when I was seven years old, and I rode my cousin Larry's bike way down on the country road passed several miles of pastures full of ponies.

Now that Spring is here, and so are the flowers, I am reminded of the many beautiful ladies we might have been fortunate to meet who are the "Mrs. Muggs" of the world. They were kind, tough as nails, made cornbread, let you pet their cats, and even gave you tomatoes.

64

THE LADY IN THE ORANGE HAT
(JANUARY 2024)

She sat next to me in the airport among the row of seats. I was on my way to Wisconsin. She was heading to Virginia. We were both going to see family members across the country. She was a short, cute, elderly Asian lady in a blue puffy coat, with a Magenta shawl around her shoulders, and a little orange hat with a white silk flower on the rim. We were both going to Denver where we would change planes. I like to call her Cai, although that is not her real name.

As we chatted, I noticed her wire rimmed glasses and smiling eyes. I complimented her on her hat, and we talked about the hats ladies used to wear in the 1950's, as her hat seemed to be from that era. Classic ladies' hats in those days were a variety of colors, such as black, white, pink, green, red, and navy with white polka dots. They were made of straw, wool felt, velvet and satin. To add that extra flair, they would be adorned with a single feather, cluster of beads, ribbons, a nylon veil netting and of course, a silk flower.

Talking to my new friend, Cai, reminded me of my mother, who often wore a hat coordinated with a smart suit, to church. As hairstyles changed in the 1950's, so did the shapes of the hats to accommodate the hair styles. There was the Velvet crescent, the Pillbox, the Beret, the Bucket, the Coolie, the Sun Hat, the Cloche and yes, the Lampshade. A woman's hat said a lot about her in those days. It mostly said that she was "classy," and "respectable."

Even men wore hats then, not baseball caps but the time-less Fedora or Trilby hat, to compliment their beautiful lean suits of muted colors. These brown hats had a tall crown and were tapered on the sides with a snap down the brim, gray binding that also said, "classy." I remember as a little girl that my dad never left our house without his brown wool felt Fedora hat, dressed in his white scrubs and tan overcoat.

I was enjoying my chat with Cai, when all too soon someone announced over the loud speaker that our flight was about to board. I helped her with her suitcase and big duffle on top of her suitcase, to get to her position in line. We smiled one last smile to say goodbye to each other, as we stepped back into the present. While some say that there is no such thing as "time travel," I beg to differ.

65

NEVER LET VISITS WITH GOOD NEIGHBORS PASS YOU BY

We all live busy lives. Some of us never see our neighbors. Some of us give them a "wave," as we pull out of our driveways. If we are fortunate to have good neighbors, they are worth our conversations. One such neighbor was, Faye, who has since passed away at 92. It would have been a very lonely time, having left my home in Texas, to move to my new home in Hermosa Beach in June 2006, if it had not been for our afternoon teas and talks on her porch.

My current neighbors are amazing former college students, now career women, who live next door to me in my neighborhood in the cute town I currently live in. We check on each other. They check on me more often, but Talia, Kim, and Caitlin have watched my cats, gotten my mail for me and have been a great comfort.

Talia has since moved away, but Kim, Caitlin and now Kelly are my "guardians" of me, in a kind way. We chat about our lives, and they seem to value the wisdom of an older woman. I think sometimes they miss their moms, and I sometimes miss my daughters, so it all evens out.

My neighbor across the street, Roni, has done the same, as she has five cats. Roni and I have gotten lunch together in town, exchanged information on plants and trees, and consulted each other on the "goings on" in our neighborhood.

My elderly neighbor, Ray, down the street, often leaves eggs from his chickens in a basket on my porch, or tomatoes from his garden. I learned the history of my neighborhood from the many stories Ray tells me, as he has lived here since he was a boy. And, his best friend, Ed, now getting along in years, shares memories of the boyhood adventures he and Ray had, climbing trees in the orange groves at the end of our street. I wish I could have seen what it all looked like then.

One can learn a lot about life, living and giving, from one's neighbors. It is what makes our neighborhoods an extension of home, an extension of "family."

66

GIRLFRIENDS

M y mom was the light of our family and I think the light in her church, as everyone knew and loved my mom. She was our "walking miracle," as she had a full recovery from a brain aneurysm in the early 1980's. She had taken my two brothers and me to church ever since we were small, but my dad, being Catholic, never went to church with us, until after my mom's miracle happened.

He must have said something to God like: "Please save her, Lord, and I'll go to church with her." God did, and he did. My dad, whom everyone knew in our town because he helped a lot of people heal from injuries and illnesses, being a physical therapist, became well known at church, too, having a servant's heart.

My mom and dad made a cute couple. He was always dressed in a suit and tie for church, and my mom always wore a dress. My dad looked out for others. When he saw a widow sitting alone, he invited her to sit with them. It turned out to be a blessing for my mom because when my dad passed away, Pauline and my mom were already best friends. And, over the years, my mom and Pauline invited other widows and sometimes couples to sit with them in church.

When I used to come home to visit my mom more often after my daughters were grown, I would go to church with her. She always went early so she could "save their pew," so all her girlfriends could sit together, a whole pew! After church, they would all go to lunch together at a place called, Bob Evans. When my mom passed away, I took her elderly girlfriends who were still around out to lunch at Bob Evans, after church. It was a bittersweet moment for me as we celebrated my mom and all the years of laughter we had shared with her.

Years later, when I became a widow, we had a widows' group at my church, so I made many friends. It still exists. Our leader, Cindy S., has hosted so many wonderful events and lunches, where friendships could develop. My friends included Sally J., Robin, and Christine, who later moved to Oregon, Florida, and Tennessee, respectively. And, over the years, I have made friends with more precious ladies, Yvonne, Cecelia, Donna, Lili, and Kathy. Other dear friends include Judy and her husband, Al; Linda and her husband, Bob; Grace and her husband, John; not to mention my Bible study gals, Donna, Gwen, Cindy G., Jackie, Shari, Linda, Barb, Sally C, and Kyna.

I realize I have become my mother now, as several of us sit in a row of chairs together at church on Sunday, close to the pulpit, so we can hear our dear Pastor Bob. Some Sundays we have lunch in our café. Other Sundays we go to our favorite hangout, Islands. And other days we go to the movies, or to concerts. I'll never be able to say enough about my sweet girlfriends, who have been there for me through heartbreaks and trials, good times and bad. It is prayer that knits us together, a common love for God, and for each other.

67

MELINA: MEETING MY ITALIAN HERITAGE

When my husband, Michael, was stricken with ALS, and lost the use of his legs, I could no longer care for him on my own. I had to put him into an assisted living facility with hospice care. I visited him most every day, especially around dinnertime, so I could help feed him. One day, as I walked into their cafeteria, there was an elderly woman feeding Michael at the table. She was caring for him like a mother would care for her son. She appeared so loving and kind.

"You'll have to excuse my mother," said a woman about my age, who looked like Sophia Loren, and was sitting nearby on a chair. "You see, my mom lost her son, my brother, a few years ago, and with her Alzheimer's she thinks your husband is her son." My heart went out to both this woman and her mother because I lost my father to Alzheimer's disease.

Melina introduced herself and we soon became great friends, as we visited our loved ones in the assisted living facility. I discovered that Melina and her mother moved from their home in Sicily, Italy, to New York City, when she was seventeen, and was living there around the same time I lived in the Big Apple. A few years later, Melina married, and moved with her husband and mother to California, and raised three sons.

As I learned of her story, how she and her mother came to America after her father died, how neither of them knew any English, I thought how brave. And, I thought, this is how my paternal grandparents came to America from Italy, not knowing any English. But they made a life here, became proud American citizens.

As we became good friends and I learned more about her life, that she still has sisters in Italy, and visits them, I began to fall more in love with my Italian heritage. How I wished my Italian father would have told me more about his parents. All I know about my grandmother, Anna, is that she came from Pescara, Italy, to America by ship when she was only nineteen years old. She was a strong swimmer and had goats. All I know about my grandfather, Patrick (Pasquale), is that he came from a little town south of Rome, called Cori, and travelled by ship to America. They both went through Ellis Island.

He then traveled from Philadelphia to Bellaire, Ohio, where he worked in the coal mines. He and my grandmother met, married, and lived in a two-story red brick house on the Ohio River. They raised my father, Joseph, his brothers, Tony, Russ, Frank and Eugene, and their sister, Lucia. Patrick died in a coal mining accident when he was only forty years old on March 19, 1931. My grandmother died from a brain embolism when my father was a sophomore in college, about the time the Japanese bombed Pearl Harbor, and he and his buddies enlisted in the Marines.

Even though my grandparents died before I was born, I felt a connection to them through Melina. But more than that, seeing her dear sweet mother made me imagine my grandmother sitting there, at the table that day. It brought tears to my eyes. Here was this dear woman, lovingly taking care of my husband, who was dying from ALS.

Melina's mother and my husband have long passed away, but she and I have a "friend connection," and a "cultural connection," through our Italian heritage. My heart longs to see where my grandparents came from, but if I never get to go, I have gotten a glimpse of them through Melina's mother's loving heart.

68

"MR. BASEBALL" GETS CALLED UP!
(REMEMBERING BOB UECKER, JANUARY 24, 2025)

I didn't know Bob Uecker very well. Most folks knew him as the "voice" of the Milwaukee Brewers for 54 seasons, and as a former professional baseball catcher who won a World Series with the Cardinals in 1964. He was also the guy who made Johnny Carson laugh hysterically on many segments on *The Tonight Show*, the actor who played character, George Owens, on the television sitcom, *Mr. Belvedere*, or the play-by-play announcer, Harry Doyle, in the movie, *Major League*, but I did get a glimpse of him through my son-in-law's eyes, Jeff Levering, who has broadcast Milwaukee Brewers' games with Bob Uecker for over a decade.

I loved how they would tell interesting stories on the air, joke with each other and laugh together. I loved how Bob would welcome my daughter, Ashley, my grandkids, and me into the press box as we tried to be quiet and watch the game. I loved how Bob would always make my grandson guess which hand he had a gumball in, then give it to him. I loved how Bob's wife, Judy, would be in there with us and we would talk quietly, trying to stifle a few laughs.

It was a rare privilege to also be in the press box when the Brewers hosted a reunion of some of the ball players who played in the 1982 World Series. It was in the press box where I got to see Bob in rare jovial form with the players, as we all partied a bit and I got to shake hands with "the kid," Robin Yount. I also had the privilege of being part of the Milwaukee Brewers' 2023 Bob Uecker "Ueck Skywalker" Star Wars Theme game, complete with "Ueck Skywalker" Star Wars Theme bobbleheads, and a tailgate party in the parking lot of American Family Field in Milwaukee.

The Brewers' ball players, manager, Pat Murphy, broadcasters, staff, and family members are like one big family, so I know they are all hurting deeply right now. And, so are the fans. No more will the players chant "UECKKKKK" and pour champagne over his head. No more will the players, like Christian Yelich, gain fatherly advice, or my son-in-law, Jeff, share stats and laughs in the press box. Bob Uecker passed away on January 16, 2025, at the age of 90, just shy of his 91st birthday, from a long battle with small cell lung cancer.

From what I understand of baseball, which isn't much, Bob's last game he announced was devastating to all involved. The Brewers, after coming "so close," to edging towards being part of the World Series, had a heartbreaking loss in the National League Wild Card series to the New York Mets in 2024. Fans most likely didn't know it at the time, that it would be "Mr. Baseball's" and their "Hall of Fame," broadcaster's last call for the team.

"Well, New York down. They did it, and the Crew will,

uh, have it end, here tonight," announced Bob Uecker. "Really crushing end to what was a fabulous end for the Milwaukee Brewers," announced Jeff Levering. "I'm telling you. That one had some sting to it," Bob followed up.

As I write this essay, a "great one," hit a home run for the Heavenly team. Can you hear it? It's the "crack of the bat!" And, he also calls it: "Get up! Get up! Get out of here! Gone!"

69

MICKY: SHE WAS A GREAT LADY

I will always remember her this way, my former sister-in-law, wonderful mother to her daughter, Michelle, and son, Brian. With my then husband, David, and her then husband, Jim, we all took the train down from New York City to Washington D.C., in the Spring of 1980 to see the cherry blossoms. The Japanese have a special word for the viewing of them, called, *hanami*. We strolled along the Tidal Basin to see the beautiful Yoshino trees on a gorgeous afternoon near the Potomac River. Micky, in beautiful "bloom" herself, at around seven months pregnant, is wearing a deep blue jumper over a white blouse. Her long brown hair is flowing in the warm breeze and she is smiling. In the background, behind her, are hundreds of pink cherry blossoms!

We were so young then, happy, free, with so many dreams and lives to build. I was racing around New York City having lunch meetings with editors when I heard the news, which I got from using a "pay telephone" in a "telephone booth," on Lexington Avenue.

A baby girl, Michelle, was born on May 23rd, big brown eyes she had, dark hair, like her beautiful mother. Years later, on May 23, 2025, in fact, Michelle, now grown, held her mother in her arms, as Micky had held her so many years ago.

In Japanese culture, the cherry blossom, "Sakura," represents renewal, love, and emotional expression. Their vibrant pink petals tell us that we need to appreciate the precious moments in life fully, as they are fleeting. The cherry blossom tree reflects the "cycle of life" to the Japanese people. If we are mindful, we can see birth, growth, peak, and eventual decline, which the Japanese accept with grace. Being a believer in the Messiah, Jesus, however, who died on the cross and rose again so we all may have eternal life, I like to believe that I will see Micky again.

Death is not the end, but the beginning of life forever wrapped in God's love in Heaven. *For God so loved the world that He gave His only Son, that whoever believes in Him, shall not perish but have eternal life. John 3:16.* And so, it is beauty and grace I see, in Micky's young face, in her hair blowing in the breeze against the background of the Sakura.

PART V

PETS ARE PEOPLE, TOO

70

THE COLOR OF LOVE

I have lived with six dogs in my life so far. Would I get another one? It is very tempting, but probably not. However, the memories of caring for them, the joy and sometimes the aggravation dogs brought into my life, is something I would not trade for the world.

My father, who was a physical therapist, had a patient whose dog, a Golden Retriever, had eight puppies. Of course, my father had to bring a puppy home when I was around two years old. Taffy was my first dog, and lived to the ripe old age of fourteen. Taffy would lie by our baby pool in the front yard and watch my brother and me as we splashed around on summer days. Our pet chickens would nestle in her fur. She was a patient soul, to the point of enduring playing "dress up" with me, as I put funny hats on her.

When we moved into our second home when I was seven years old, Taffy followed my two younger brothers everywhere as they played "cowboys" or "army," going around the neighborhood with their friends. One day, as the summer was drawing to a close, she disappeared. We were devastated. A new school year began, and I found it hard to concentrate in my class. All I could think about was my beloved Taffy. Where did she go? Would I ever see her again? Two weeks later, a miracle happened. She appeared on our front lawn one morning, as if she had always been there. We figured someone she went home with had a change of heart for a heartbroken family.

My brother, John, later got Jessie, another Golden Retriever, shortly after Taffy crossed over the "Rainbow Bridge." One day, when Jessie was a puppy, he was in the kitchen. Our mom opened a bottom drawer and out popped a roll of aluminum foil, making a racket as it rolled across the floor. I think it scared Jessie for life. Every time our mom wanted him out of the kitchen, she just opened that drawer and Jessie would run!

When we all got older, my father learned to fly private airplanes and went in with several friends to purchase one. Often, my dad would fly by himself. I sensed it was his escape, a chance to feel free for a while. But one day, he started taking Jessie with him and Jessie "loved" to fly! Our dad would always say: "Jessie is my best copilot!" Jessie also loved sleeping at the foot of my parents' bed, and crossed the "Rainbow Bridge" on my brother John's wedding day, at age thirteen.

Several years later, my then husband, David, and I raced up to Poughkeepsie, New York, from Mt. Kisco, after we bought our first home, to get the last yellow Labrador Retriever puppy in a litter. We named him, Sunny. He walked with me everywhere in our quiet neighborhood. He loved running in the woods with our friends' German Shepherd, Tiffany, who was a surprise wedding present for our friends Joy and Howland.

A year later, Sunny was pacing with me in our family room as I walked back and forth, in labor, with my oldest daughter, Lindsay. He did not much like being replaced by a new baby in a car seat, as Sunny was used to being the baby that went to pick up daddy at the train station. But he and Lindsay became great pals, as she would feed him snow from her toy spoon when we had snow storms in winter, or let him play in her baby pool in the summertime.

Sunny loved our new home near San Francisco, as we moved when my second daughter, Ashley, was a baby. He enjoyed ramming right through our screen door as he raced up the backyard hill to see his "deer girlfriend," waiting to play with him on the other side of our six-foot fence! Sunny made a few "skunk friends," too. We soon learned other uses for milk and tomato juice!

When Sunny was eleven years old, we got him a sister, Laina, another yellow Labrador Retriever. Sunny loved her so much he would grab toys and shake them in front of her face so she would play with him. They were both great protectors of our golden, lop-eared bunny, Fluffy, as the three of them would sit at the top of the hill starring down at us through our kitchen window as we ate our breakfast.

Sunny crossed over the "Rainbow Bridge," on the same day as Princess Diana passed away, when we lived in Texas. And, Laina crossed over the "Rainbow Bridge" when my daughters were both at college. We put the cell phone to her ear, so my daughters could say goodbye to their beloved Laina. We all cried our eyes out. I missed my walking buddy for a long time.

Charley, my Cavalier King Charles, was my *Travels With Charley*, by John Steinbeck, dog. He was as hyper as he was dear, traveling with me in my silver PT Cruiser from Texas to Hermosa Beach, California. He was my "friend maker," my companion, during some very lonely, difficult days, as we walked beside the ocean together on The Strand.

Then, there was Shadow, who had the head of a German Shepherd, the body of a long-haired Dachshund and a tail like a fox. She was so happy when I came into the family of my second husband, Michael, and his sons. We girls stuck together, as I knew how important it was to get a good grooming now and then. Makes a girl feel special. At seventeen years of age, we had to say goodbye to Shadow, my little shadow. Even my four cats, Tyson, Hannah, Oscar, and Lucy missed her.

So, what's the point of my telling you about my dogs? They were golden, brown, black and white. We loved them because of their character, their unconditional love, a sweetness that has no color really. And dogs don't see colors either. Maybe that's why they are the color of love.

71

PETS MAKE THE WORLD GO 'ROUND

W hen my kids were growing up, I always made sure to spend "one-on-one" time with each of them every week. We always had a blast. Sometimes, those days were dangerous, as in, we sometimes ended up going to the pet store and buying a pet. Often, famous last words would be: "Just looking!" And a "*please* mommy," often made my heart cave.

When my younger daughter, Ashley, spotted a tiny ball of golden fur in a cage, of course, we had to get, Fluffy, our little lop-eared bunny. She became the mascot of our two Labrador Retrievers who adored her. I never had to worry about the hawks getting Fluffy, when Sunny and Laina were protecting her on the hill in our backyard. One morning, as were eating breakfast in our kitchen, there was Fluffy, at the top of our backyard hill, sitting between Sunny and Laina, all looking down at us. If she was playing in the bushes all day, she always came to our backdoor at dinnertime, with our two dogs.

When I took my older daughter, Lindsay, to the pet store another time, we got Herbie, a black, brown, and white guinea pig. Somehow, my daughters were willing to share Fluffy, but when Ashley saw Herbie, we had to go right back to the pet store and get Pumpkin. We all enjoyed many hours feeding them carrots and watching them wander through the grass. Then, there were the yellow baby ducks I got from the farmers' market. My daughters named them Daisy and Maisy. They played in part of the yard we fenced in that included a kiddie pool. My daughters loved holding their ducks, who were quite tame. This went well until Daisy and Maisy grew huge and white. I had to chase them around their play yard every night to bring them into the garage so the skunks would not get them. They later took a nice trip back to the farm from whence they were hatched, and a big lake. We learned to say "goodbye," as they happily swam away.

And, of course, we had some lizards, chameleons. One got stuck under my daughter, Lindsay's bed, somehow. But we rescued him. It was later that tragedy struck, when our dogs, Sunny, and Laina, got fleas. We had to fumigate the house, so I put the lizards in their aquarium under a shady tree in the backyard. The only problem was, the sun moved. "You fried our lizards!" Lindsay yelled. Oops. I profusely apologized and tried to comfort my daughters. I think I referenced, "The Circle of Life."

Following in our family tradition, my daughter, Ashley, spent the day with her eight-year-old son, Brock, a couple years back. Somehow, they wandered into a pet store and bought, Rupert, a betta fish. Well, Ashley and Brock got him settled into his new home, a small aquarium. Brock wrote out a schedule when to feed Rupert, and clean his home once a week. He was even willing to allow his sister, Logan, five years old at the time, to have a turn feeding him. Prone to fighting occasionally, this was a golden opportunity for my daughter to explain: "You know, bettas *must* have a 'calm environment,'" she said, as her kids nodded their heads in unison.

So, pets teach us how to love creatures big and small; how to care for them; how to eventually say, "goodbye," and how to work out disagreements calmly. As my daughter, Ashley, walked away, she heard Brock tell Logan: "So, that means no fighting with each other, okay Logan?" Nod.

72

OUR CATS AND JAY LENO

"Mom, may I *please* get a cat?" my daughter, Ashley, begged me when she was thirteen years old. Her older sister, Lindsay, figuring she was allergic to cats, immediately piped up: "Can we just get a dog that *looks* like a cat?"

Since our family never had a cat before, and I never had a cat growing up, I did some investigating about cats and allergies. When I consulted with a naturopathic doctor I was seeing, she suggested getting a product called, *Green Miracle* from *Ultimate Living*. The year was 1999, and this product was developed by a lady who had breast cancer, which helped put her in remission as far as I know. It was a green powdery mixture and they later came out with the same type of mixture for pets. It had a lot of healthy greens in it. The idea was, that if you could neutralize a cat's saliva, which contained the "protein" that may cause allergic reactions in people, then you could have a cat in your home, minus the watery eyes and stuffy nose.

So, I found a lady from a no kill animal shelter who was

fostering a litter of kittens. Ashley and I went to see the lady at her home. When Ashley sat on the floor to play with the kittens, a cute orange tabby walked over to her and crawled into her lap. "What's this kitten's name?" Ashley asked the foster mom. "Sunny!" she replied. Ashley and I looked at each other, astonished. We had just lost our first dog, Sunny, who had recently passed away.

Later renamed, Tyson, he was our joy, and loved playing with our dog, Laina. It was so funny to watch them play together, as Tyson would grab Laina's neck with his little paws and she would shake him off, run around in a circle and come back for more. When they took a nap together, it was Tyson who put his paws over Laina's paws, claiming her for his own.

As the years rolled by and my daughters went off to college, I adopted a part Siamese, part tabby cat and named her, Hannah. She had gorgeous blues eyes and a gray and white coat. She and Tyson became husband and wife. Later, I found my beloved, Lucy, a white domestic shorthair, who had an enormous personality and loved everyone. All my cats seemed to adopt a bit of the habits of our dog, Laina. Lucy, especially, would always greet me at the door when I came home.

In June 2006, when I moved to Hermosa Beach, California, it was a very lonely time, even though I had my three cats, and my Cavalier King Charles, Charley. A glutton for animals, I was at the vet with one of my cats and spied a gorgeous Flame Point Siamese kitten, Oscar. His amazing blue eyes, sand colored coat and gentle personality captured my heart. I decided Lucy needed a friend and so they became husband and wife. My pet family was complete.

For my fifty-third birthday, my two daughters, Lindsay and Ashley, also living near me, decided to take me to a comedy club where Jay Leno was performing.

We had great seats, right next to the stage. As Jay was warming up the audience, he asked various questions. Wouldn't you know, it would have to do with cats!

"How many of you have one cat?" he asked. My hand went up. "How many of you have two cats?" Jay continued. Again, my hand went up. "How many of you have three cats?" he persisted. My hand went up, as the audience began to laugh. "How many of you have four cats?" he asked one more time. And, my hand went up. "Yep, you're single!" he exclaimed, amid much laughter.

Yes, I was the single cat lady! In my wildest dreams I never thought I would have four amazing cats, and I dearly loved them all. They became my family, in the love they gave me during my times of loneliness in being single, during my married life, and later in being a widow. I will forever be grateful that my daughter, Ashley, asked: "Mom, may I *please* get a cat?"

73

WHERE DID ALL THE REAL
DOGS GO?

When I was a small child, my father brought home a Golden Retriever puppy. We named her Taffy. She was not a Golden Doodle, but a real Golden Retriever and she was awesome. Not to poo-poo owners of "designer dogs," but if I wanted to buy a dog today, it would be like going through fifty different meal items at my favorite restaurant, or trying to decide what movie to watch with a choice of 500 channels on my television set.

How does one choose? Are there any good old fashioned Irish Setters, or regular sized German Shepherds, or standard Poodles? I would not want a mini or maxi or companion size dog. Just give me those dogs we used to have. Come to think of it, I have not seen any full-size Collies, or "Lassies," for years. They have gone into the "history zone," like Buffy, my grandfather George's Cocker Spaniel, who used to fetch his slippers the minute he sat down in his easy chair at night.

It seems the designer dog business has been booming

over the past several years. A designer dog, by definition, means it is a "mixed breed," dog created by crossbreeding two purebred dogs to create a hybrid with desired traits. It is sort of like, instead of drinking *Folgers* coffee, you can now get a café mocha or a nonfat latte. Buffy's descendants are Cockapoos, now, which sounds like some sort of exotic bird!

Yes, there are now unlimited options of designer dogs. You can have a hypoallergenic dog, or a smaller Golden Retriever, or a dog mix of a Chihuahua and a Yorkshire Terrier, which sounds like the size of my once beloved guinea pig, Dusty. But, if I was going to get a dog today, I would still get a good old Golden Retriever that sheds because this breed conjures up such fond memories for me. When my mom used to clean up all of Taffy's dog hair rolling across the floor as big as tumble weeds, she used to say: "We have enough dog hair around here for another dog!" Maybe *that's* where they all come from!

74

WHO TOOK THE HAM?

When I was a kid, my mom used to leave a frozen chicken or a roast out to thaw so they would be ready to cook for dinner. Even in the summertime. No one ever got sick. Everyone did that and it was fine. Well one summer's day, my mom left a ham on the kitchen table to thaw while she took my two brothers and me to the park to play.

We left our dog, Taffy, our beautiful Golden Retriever, sleeping quite content, in a sunny spot in the kitchen. We never had to worry about her because she never jumped up on a table or couch. She was perfectly happy to accept table scraps that might end up on the floor. And, she loved Friday nights when my mom let us have potato chips and soda when we watched our favorite TV show, *The Flintstones*. We snuck chips to her when our mom was not looking.

So, we come home from our day at the park and my mom shrieks: "Where did my ham go?" Then, turning to us she inquires: "I left it on the table, right?" We all nodded, yes.

Suddenly, my brother, Dan, says: "I see something!" We followed a trail of grease around the corner and who should we see but our gluttonous dog, Taffy. She ate the whole ham! Taffy, of course, looks up at us with her guilty eyes, like dogs do, and sheepishly lies back down on her rug. After things settled down, since our dad was out of town on a fishing trip, my mom took us to McDonald's.

We forgave Taffy. She was such a sweet dog and never did anything like that again. After she crossed the "Rainbow Bridge," my brother, John, found Jessie, another Golden Retriever. We kept a better eye on him, although he got table scraps sometimes, and toast when we watched out favorite Saturday cartoons, like *Wile E. Coyote and Road Runner*.

One day, Jessie was bugging our mom in the kitchen when she was cooking. She opened the bottom drawer to get out the aluminum foil and lost her grip on the roll. Well, the roll popped out of the drawer and the aluminum foil rolled out over the kitchen floor. Jessie freaked out! He could not get out of our kitchen fast enough. So, for years after this incident, anytime our mom wanted to get Jessie out of her kitchen, she just opened that drawer and he was gone! "Beep! Beep!" Just like Road Runner.

75

SAYING GOODBYE TO LUCY

She was twenty years old in human years, ninety-six years old in cat years, and there was never a person who came into my home that she did not greet and grab with her little paw to elicit some affection. My white domestic shorthair cat, Lucy, whose name means, "light," was truly an unusual cat. She was raised with dogs, so she woke me every morning at six o'clock, and greeted me at the backdoor every time I arrived home.

Lucy was the friendliest of my cats, so full of life and spunk, always climbing on the cat trees to be among my huge plants in our kitchen sunroom. When a girlfriend helped me move from Texas to California, I thought I had almost lost her, but she had crawled up inside this recliner in our hotel room, where we found her.

One by one I have had to say goodbye to my other cats, and dogs, but Lucy was my last pet. She loved sitting on the back porch with me as I drank my coffee and we enjoyed the morning sunshine. She loved sitting next to me when I watched television, and loved to grab my hand with her little paw and pull it closer. She was my little snuggle bug, my constant companion.

She got me outside to listen to the birds. She helped me slow down and smell the roses. Towards the last two days of her life with me, we took naps together and she again grabbed my hand to pull it closer, her way of saying, "I love you." She was so strong for being so weak. She looked at me a long time as if to say, "I'm going to miss you, too, but I'll be waiting for you in Heaven."

She knew my tears and looked at me as if to say: "It's okay, mom. It's my time to go." I kissed her forehead and let her go. For the first time since 1982, I do not have a pet in my life. They all brought me such joy, every one, and especially, my Lucy.

76

CADY AND RILEY: A TRIBUTE

"Mom, can I get her, *please!*" Ashley begged, this time, for a Puggle puppy, she named, Cady. It was probably not the best time to get a dog, but we are suckers for animals in our family. Who could resist this fawn-colored cutie with the dark brown eyes?

Ashley was a sophomore in college living in an apartment with two roommates, but was more responsible than I would have guessed. She took good care of her puppy, even in times of great stress to herself. One night she called me crying: "Mom, Cady keeps barking at night. I can't sleep! I have finals coming up! I can't take this!" I would try to console her as best I could. Having a new "baby" while going to college was not the best time to have a puppy, but it all worked out.

When Ashley graduated and had a full-time job, she always came home on her lunch hour to take Cady out for a walk. When she and her husband, Jeff, married, Cady became their joint first child and she was loved. They often threw the ball for her and took her on walks. Cady went from living in California to Missouri to Massachusetts to Wisconsin as Jeff got bigger job opportunities. She was loved when their two human kids came along, loved by Brock and Logan, loved when she went blind and loved to the very end. While the kids were at school and Jeff and Ashley took Cady to the vet to say goodbye, she passed away in Jeff's arms, as if to say: "I know you got me, dad. Thank you for being mine."

My oldest daughter, Lindsay, was a working girl when Ashley and I convinced her to get an adorable Boston Terrier puppy, she named, Riley. If ever there was a more spoiled Hollywood star, it was Riley. Dressed in all sorts of outfits, taken everywhere with her, Lindsay adored Riley. She was rambunctious, sweet, and quite the "dog about town." Riley traveled many places by airplane, including to the house I grew up in, as we all shared one last Christmas together before my mom passed away. And again, Riley was dressed up in a cute outfit, ready for the holidays. She made Christmas that year extra special.

Little did we know that Riley, at two years of age, had a heart defect, and passed away in Lindsay's arms. I raced up from my home an hour away to be with her. I think the saddest part of having a pet is when they die suddenly, and there is nothing you can do about it. But I do believe that all our pets reside in Heaven, waiting for us, and will one day say: "What took you so long? Let's play!"

77

MY DAUGHTER GOT A HORSE NAMED, ROY!

He is not really a horse. He is a Bernese Mountain dog. My daughter, Ashley, had always wanted a "big" dog! I do not know if any dog comes any bigger before it is called a Shetland pony. Maybe a Mastiff.

"I thought we were getting a puppy!" my grandson, Brock, wondered. My granddaughter, Logan, was bewildered too, as Roy, at nine weeks of age, weighed a hefty twenty-six pounds! They were used to their much smaller Puggle, Cady, I'm guessing. But they quickly fell in love with Roy. Everyone did, including all the neighbors.

The Bernese Mountain dog originates from Switzerland, around the Swiss Alps. It does have ancestral roots in the Roman Mastiff. All I know is that Roy, now at one year of age and weighing in at 110 pounds, has really been enjoying his "first snowfall" in the Midwest, and hates to come into the house. My daughter had to take him out on his leash when the temperature dropped below zero this past winter, for five minutes only, so they both did not freeze.

Roy is a gentle dog, and was very popular when all the family members got together for this past Christmas holiday. He would just lie quietly on the floor when my three-year-old granddaughter, Brynn, cuddled with him, as if he was an old blanket. She reminded me of a "stern," little Shirley Temple if Roy got to be too much for her. Brynn would let him know she was the boss: "Sit, Roy!" she would say. "Back, Roy!"

Roy does not play "fetch," but he likes to lop around the house like a bear who just ate too much honey. He gets a moment of the "zoomies," first thing in the morning, a wild burst of energy, and that is it for the rest of the day.

He loves to play "guard dog," though, and when the weather is nice, he will sit in the yard, surrounded by an invisible fence, and greet all the neighbors. Most everyone knows Roy, and they will say, "hi, Roy," when they are on their daily walks around the neighborhood. So, I guess you could say that Roy is the "town greeter." He likes that job most of all.

He loves waiting with my grandkids as they wait for the school bus each morning. He loves waiting for them to get off the school bus when they come home in the afternoon. They love to run up and hug him. He is his mama's constant companion; his father's greeter after a long business trip. He is the "keeper of the family flame." He is Roy.

78

ALL PETS HAVE A PURPOSE, I THINK
(SEPTEMBER 2024)

"He started out as a little guy on my shoulder, then, when he got to be four feet long and started sunning himself on the windowsill, I had to have a talk with my son," said my friend, Cindy. As Cindy, Yvonne, Beth, and I were eating lunch at our quaint local diner, our conversation had drifted to pets we have known. The pet Cindy was referring to was her son's lizard, Cecil.

Cecil eventually moved to a new home and as far as we know, lived "happily ever after." It made me think of all the pets my mom let my brothers and I have. It also made me think of all the pets I let my kids have, and the pets they have now. Years ago, we had a milkman and an egg man, who delivered milk and eggs to our doorstep. The milk came in brown glass bottles. It was the egg man, a local farmer, who had baby bunnies one day, and that's how I got my pet rabbit, Marshmallow.

It was also the egg man who gave us our pet chicken, Toby. My dad hung a swing in our basement, and when my brother, Dan, and I played "swinging cowboys and Indians," in our fancy outfits, Toby would run around the basement with us. Years later, when we moved to a bigger house, my mom let us have fish, Swordtails. What an experience that was, as my two brothers and I watched in horror as these fish ate their own babies as fast as they popped out of the mother fish! We did manage to save a few of them.

Later, my brother, John, had a snake, that we think died of old age. When I was in second grade, my principal had two guinea pigs he was giving away in a contest. "You can bring one home if you win it and it's not pregnant," my mom told me. Well, guess what? I was delighted around Christmastime, to have four more guinea pigs!

Our Golden Retriever, Taffy, always joined our Friday night potato chip and soda parties during our favorite TV show, *The Flintstones*. Our second Golden Retriever, Jessie, loved to go jogging in Groby's Field with me. My daughters, Ashley and Lindsay loved our Labrador Retrievers, Sunny, and Laina, as they all enjoyed playing, "dress up." Their guinea pigs, Pumpkin and Herbie, provided many delightful hours of fun with eating carrots and roaming in the backyard grass. And, Fluffy, just like our Taffy, though a bunny, loved laying in between my daughters on the floor, as they watched "their" favorite TV show, *Are You Afraid of The Dark?*

In addition, my kids had lizards, two ducks, three cats; and later two dogs each, Cady and Riley, in their early adult years. Ashley, currently, is enjoying her horse, a Bernese Mountain dog, named Roy. And, whenever my three-year-old granddaughter Brynn, her mom, Lindsay, and dad, Shawn, travel to visit Shawn's dad, Gary, she plays with Poppy, a beautiful Golden Retriever. Funny how the "circle of pets" continues throughout our lives, in the lives of our kids and grandkids.

For the first time in my life, I am "pet less." It feels strange not to see my beautiful white cat, Lucy, greet me at the backdoor when I come home. Sometimes, I enjoy the quiet. Sometimes, the quiet is too much. But I am grateful. Pets are the companions and educators of our lives. No doubt about it.

PART VI

PLACES TO BE; THINGS TO DO

79

WHEN SUMMERS WERE SIMPLE

I was thinking the other day about movies that take place in the summer, like *Rear Window, A Summer Place, Gidget, American Graffiti.* These are the movies that remind me of summer fun when I was a kid and teenager, like a summer vacation our family spent on Lake Gage, in Indiana, in 1971. In my heart I am remembering a summer crush on a blonde-haired boy with blue eyes who drove a red Fiat, strolls around the lake with my mother, and her teaching me how to crochet during the lazy afternoons on the screened in porch, while my father and brothers were off fishing. I remember writing poems about sailboats catching the wind in their sails, warm breezes on my face, and sunsets that lit up the sky.

I remember my mother giving us summer passes for our community swimming pool where my brothers, our friends and I would hang out all day. Our mom would pick us up around dinnertime and take us to this place called, Sandy's, to get hamburgers, French Fries, and cokes. The burgers cost only fifteen cents. An avid reader, I would always have a book in my hand. That summer, after my junior year in high school, I think it was, *The Catcher in The Rye*, by J.D. Salinger.

I remember playing miniature golf with friends and then going to the drive-in movie theatre next door. I once got a hole in one and was so proud of myself. I had a boyfriend with the bluest eyes I had ever seen, whom I met at my brothers' Boy Scout camp. We went steady for a summer, then drifted apart by autumn.

My mind rambles back to when I was six years old sitting on the porch with my mother, snapping green beans, when the air was filled with butterflies, before pesticides. Barbecue grills became the rage and men became expert grill masters with steaks or burgers or hot dogs.

I remember a park called, Lakeside, that had a small lake and rides for kids, like the carousel. I can still see my dad's open hand, holding quarters, as I begged him to let me have one more ride on the carousel. He always did. And, I remember my first experience in a greenhouse on the grounds of the Dayton Veterans Administration Center in Dayton, Ohio. A history of the Center was written by my grandfather, Chaplain George L. Cutton, in 1950. When my mother took us inside of this greenhouse, I felt transported to another place. The huge green tropical plants, the pond with a small ball of synchronized moving golden fish, was enchanting! And, looking up through the glass to the blue sky and white clouds above made me feel like all was right in my world! It was a time when a loving heart felt, before the mind could think.

80

CLOTHES HOLD OUR MEMORIES

A few years ago, when my oldest daughter, Lindsay, was single, I was helping her discard clothes and pack up her things for a future move to a new apartment. This is how it all went, one sunny summer afternoon, as the salty air of the ocean blew through the curtains.

We are in her closet, which sort of reminds me of a big hot air balloon, so full of air that if you stuck it with a pin, everything would explode! Who wants to remember to discard the clothes we should have discarded a long time ago? "You can have this," my daughter says, as she tackles this jungle of clothes. I am happy. One woman's disaster is another woman's treasure.

All afternoon we put various clothes in piles: keep; give to mom; give away. Isn't this what we do with the memories that belong to the clothes? Some clothes we want to keep because they remind us of good memories. Some clothes we discard because the memories are just too painful.

Once, when I was going through a difficult time in my

life, I asked a friend if those painful memories ever go away. She told me that when I had replaced enough sad memories with happy memories that the sad ones would fade away.

Today, my daughter and I discard memories that I think are too painful for me, because I remember a time in my life when I bought those clothes for her. Maybe they are too painful for her, too, but we just converse in idle chit-chat, and smile, as we look through the clothes. Some clothes are just too personal to talk about.

But then, I remember all the baby clothes that are still in a big bag in my closet that I will never give away. Currently, Lindsay is expecting her second daughter. We were at my home in my garage, not long ago, and I found the little terry cloth outfit, yellow and white, with a pink ice cream cone on the chest, that was her first outfit as a newborn. "Look at this!" I show her, as she takes it from me and holds it up in her hands. "Wow," she replies. "I was so tiny!" Faster than a second in my mind I am holding my newborn daughter in her outfit in the summer of 1983. I marvel at her delicate face, her tiny hands, and fingers. Suddenly, I am singing and dancing with her in our living room, my precious one, for a moment in time...

Sometimes, clothes are the memories we keep forever in our hearts. Sometimes, clothes are the memories that we must give away. And, sometimes, we need to make space for new clothes.

81

"IF I NEED IT, I GOT IT!"

When my two brothers and I were growing up we lived in a ranch style home that had a crawlspace underneath the house. As young kids, we used to play in the crawlspace and pretend it was our "hide out." As the years moved on, our father, who was a product of the Great Depression, saved "everything!"

No paint can, bag of cement, electric motor, old medical journal, board of lumber, fishing pole, folding vinyl partition, or toilet seat ever had to worry about being thrown out. Once they made it into the crawlspace, they were safe for all eternity! Our father's motto was: "If I need it, I got it!"

There was also a blue plastic baby bathtub, pipes, boxes of nails and screws, and assorted toys, never to be played with again. There was a wooden door to the crawlspace that was painted white, with a hook to close it. As time marched on, various leaves and spider webs guarded the entrance protected by cement walls. We grew up and forgot about all the stuff in that crawlspace. When our father passed away, it was his forgotten domain, almost a memorial to all the things he made with his hands, all the things he fixed, all the things he saved for some "rainy day."

I had long forgotten about the crawlspace until I was talking to a girlfriend of mine, who was beside herself, buried in piles of papers and junk filling up their home that her husband had no desire to deal with. We talked about what she could do with all the piles. "Make it a date night thing!" I suggested. "Play some fun music and the two of you can sort it all into smaller piles: keep, donate, throw away." But she looked at me dumbfounded.

Then I asked her: "What items are "special" to you, in all those piles?" She mentioned photographs, and some other trinkets. I then thought about some things that were special to me, that I had collected in my home: a box of postcards my mom, who passed away years ago, had written to family members and friends from all the vacation places she traveled to with my dad. I thought about her eye glasses I have kept, and an olive-colored box that she kept her little brush curlers and bobby pins in. I thought about a receipt from the Dayton Biltmore Hotel, where my parents spent their first night as a married couple. The bill was eight dollars.

I have no qualms about throwing junk away. It is so easy nowadays to think that: "If I need it, I'll just go get it!" How simple are our "throw away" lives? And, what is considered "junk," anyway? Maybe it is the treasures that we keep, the treasures that we always and only just remember, or the treasures we need that we wish we had kept.

82

RIDING THE WAVES OF LAUGHTER

My toddler granddaughter, Brynn, is most interesting in that she laughs all the time. I have never met a child who is so cheerful, and I hope and pray that life will always be safe and wonderful for her, for all my grandkids. We played all day one day with putting together puzzles, kicking balls around, dancing.

She has this little book that plays different musical tunes with singing. And the song she loves to play is, *Baby Shark*. Well, she starts playing the song and swaying to the music. And I don't know what came over me, but I love to dance, so I was doing this crazy dance. She starts laughing and laughing and laughing, which made me laugh, too. My daughter, Lindsay, comes into the bedroom and starts laughing.

We were all laughing so hard we couldn't stop. We kept playing the song and laughing. I have never heard a baby laugh so much. It just made my day, and my daughter's day.

Such a joy can hardly be described except to relate to what one person once said: "Laughter is an instant vacation!" Indeed, it is.

83

INVENTIONS MAKE THE WORLD GO 'ROUND TOO FAST

I n 1913, an American engineer by the name of Fred Wolf, completely changed the way we lived when he designed and patented the electric refrigerator. It revolutionized the way we bought and stored food. They were built so well years ago, that I do not think we had to replace our refriger-ator my parents bought in 1961, for twenty years.

In 1927, Philo Farnsworth invented the first television set. And, for the first time in history, we could see significant historical events as they were taking place. I remember inter-viewing the famous Olympic gold medal winner in freestyle swimming, Ann Curtis, years ago. Curtis participated in the 1948 London Olympics, the first Summer Games in twelve years, after WWII. She told me that she was invited to a dinner by Queen Elizabeth and was surprised to learn about television. As they were discussing her events, Curtis said the Queen remarked: "The buoys were larger than I thought they'd be," "What do you mean?" Curtis asked. "I saw them on the telly!" the Queen replied.

When color television came out, as kids, my brothers and I had a choice, green faces or pink. I always liked black and white television better. But, today, of course, the colors on televisions are remarkable.

On December 17, 1903, the Wright brothers, Orville and Wilbur, flew successfully with their invention, the airplane, which made flight possible. I remember the first time I flew on an airplane when I was five years old with my family. We went to my cousin's wedding in Washington DC. It was a roomy *TWA* airplane, and we had an amazing flight. People dressed up. The flight attendants served you yummy meals and gave us kids *TWA* pins.

In 1971, the *Kenbak-1* personal computer came out. The *Kenbak* Corporation only sold forty units initially, and folded two years later. But soon *Apple's* PC came along, and they sold about six million units between 1977 and 1993. I remember making that "giant leap of faith" from my *Corona* typewriter to my first computer in order to write my first book. It took time getting used to it, but made typing go so much faster.

In 1983, the internet was invented. Sadly, letter writing became a lost art, as emails were much easier and faster to send to people. But I still write letters sometimes, and I have kept all the very special letters of my family members over the years. Yes, inventions have made life easier and faster and more efficient. But there are days that I dream about riding a train across this great country of ours, writing postcards along the way, as I gaze out at the beautiful mountains and plains passing swiftly by.

84

GOING TO PRESCHOOL MAKES ME
FEEL LIKE A KID AGAIN

I nstead of "preschool," they should call it, "play school." I
had a chance recently to vicariously experience life as a
kid through my granddaughter Brynn's eyes, at her amazing
preschool. It looked like a "Garden of Eden," where kids
mostly play outside all day beneath lemon trees near a small
waterfall and sandy miniature beach.

I sat with a couple of moms, who at first, thought I was
my granddaughter's mom, until my daughter, Lindsay, introduced us. Thank you, ladies. My daughter left to go get some
work done at her home office, so I stayed and watched my
granddaughter have the time of her life.

A total "water dog," at heart, my granddaughter went
straight for the kid sized sink to play with the water. Next,
she darted to the play house where the kids decided to move
the doll bed and chairs outside. Then, she went over to the
huge artist's canvas on a table where cans of blue paint were
open all around for the kids to paint on the canvas.

When my daughter later texted me, I joyfully could

proclaim that "her daughter," yes indeed, looked like a blue painting all over her pink shorts and top! A brief time later, a gate leading to the sand cave and tiny waterfall was opened so the kids could wander onto a small sandy beach and play with lots of water. They got buckets full of water from a little stream and poured it into a big pot to make something.

My granddaughter later found a tree stump with steps leading up to it, which she loved climbing on and then jumping off into sand, barefoot. Next, came clean up time, hand washing and snack time. The kids went to two tables, while the teachers passed out snacks and cups of water. My granddaughter, who is lean, very active, and always hungry, ate the last remaining rice cake nobody wanted.

Climbing activities on a little hill followed, then some story time. I thought the teacher did a very good job telling stories with felt cut outs on a board to keep their attention. Some of the kids wanted to take the felt cut outs off the board and examine them thoroughly, my granddaughter included.

Clean up songs were followed by goodbye songs, as the teacher sang goodbye to every child who wanted their name included in the song. Mothers soon arrived and began gathering their kids' belongings, such as shoes, backpacks, water bottles. Some of the children's mothers put them in fresh clean clothes if their fun old clothes had become unrecognizable. Brynn ran to her mom when she saw her, and Lindsay changed her into fresh clean clothes.

My granddaughter had so much fun she only came up to me twice during our play time to show me a doll or give me her *Crocs*, as she wanted to go barefoot, which was allowed and encouraged. Soon she was ready to go home with us, having played nicely with all the other kids.

As I watched her having fun running barefoot, playing with water, painting her shirt blue, singing, and listening to stories, I thought of the bestseller from years ago, *All I Really Need to Know I Learned in Kindergarten*, by Robert Fulghum. I figure this age-old wisdom can apply to preschool, too.

85

NEVER UNDERESTIMATE THE WHERE-WITH-ALL OF A THREE-YEAR-OLD

My granddaughter, Brynn, goes to music class one day a week. When she is home, she loves to grab her little pink plastic guitar in the living room, sit on the ottoman in her "Jamamas," which are her pajamas, and sing you all the songs she knows, which are a lot.

She wants you to participate, too, when she claps her hands, just like her favorite music teacher, Miss Melanie. "Brynn is the 'teacher's pet,'" my daughter, Lindsay, tells me, about her precocious daughter. "She loves to sit in the teacher's lap during music time. It's 'her spot!'"

One morning, when Brynn came to music class, she saw that a "new girl" had taken her spot in the teacher's lap. Rather than cry or get upset about it, though, my granddaughter got an idea. She decided to go sit in the lap of the new girl's mother. The new girl saw Brynn sitting in her mother's lap and immediately got off the teacher's lap and ran to her mother, to sit in her mother's lap. Brynn immediately gets up and runs to sit in the lap of her teacher. Problem solved.

86

MY FIRST PICKLEBALL LESSON
(AUGUST 2023)

I was a tad bit apprehensive but excited, to take my first pickleball lesson with Rick, a professional tennis and pickleball player, and fantastic coach. A very patient guy, he is all about "strategy."

He started me out with "dinks." First, I hit the ball upwards slightly over and over with my paddle to get the feel of the ball hitting the paddle. You always want to make sure you hit the ball with the "center" of the paddle. This tip made sense to me, because if you get "centered," in life, going forward is always easier.

Next, I practiced dinking the ball just over the net to Rick. You want to dink upwards slightly with your paddle so it goes over the net but into the "no-volley zone," because it is then harder for your opponent to hit it. This strategy reminds me that sometimes, "less is more," in the game of life.

Next, he had me practice serving the ball. I stood in the right side of my court, and like tennis, I served it over the net to the opposite corner into the opponent's court. No one was there, of course, but Rick set up "markers" so I would hit the ball past them into the court corner. "Keep your wrist straight, look at the ball, not the court, hit the ball high and far," instructed Rick. "Aim the paddle where you want your ball to go." This tip made sense because when you hit a "high serve," to the back of your opponent's court, he has to run farther back and it will be more difficult for him to hit the ball as it must "bounce first." It's sort of like when you take the "high road," your opposing subject doesn't know what to do.

It took me a minute to get my bearings, but I hit several balls high into the opposite corner. "Now, when it's windy, you're going to want to do a 'drive serve,' which is lower," explained Rick. Yes, I thought, like when the storms of life come at us, we want to "drive on," be strong, not let things get us down.

So, I practiced and gained more self-confidence and realized, hey, I can do this! And, it's a blast! In fact, it's downright addicting, but in a good way. And, I didn't mind getting up at 6:00 am to go on a beautiful drive as the sun was shining to take my lesson with Rick. Other players were on other courts, having fun, laughing, enjoying their lives.

Wow, I thought, it just feels great to learn a new skill and play pickleball. Not so much because I'm competitive and love strategies, but with all that's going on in the world, whether it's a song, or a community coming together to help each other, playing pickleball gives me the feeling that somehow by living my life, I'm holding onto my freedom. Because when we are "deliberate" with our lives, it is then we can truly "live" our lives.

87

A SALUTE TO MOTHERS, AS THEIR KIDS GO BACK TO SCHOOL (FOR ASHLEY)

When did the kitchen faucet start dripping, and the washing machine become so loud? Where did that bird come from, singing outside my window? And, when did the mint in my flower pot on the windowsill grow so high? I gaze outside at the backyard at my children playing on their swings, but they are not there. They are at school – all day.

I sip coffee from my cup with their pictures on it, and keep gazing out the window. How is it my heart aches so, from already missing them? How could I have wanted the summer to end, so I could get some peace and quiet? I busy myself, tidying up their rooms, feeding Rupert the fish in his aquarium, the one we got after so many trips to the pet store as my son begged me for a fish. I hang his clean baseball uniform in his closet. I sew a button on my daughter's now worn-out favorite summer dress. And, I sit, thinking.

Is this what peace and quiet is, alone in my house? The quiet is so quiet. Then, the tears trickle down my cheeks as I remember the days at the swimming pool, the trips to the zoo, the vacation by the lake, the county fair...that went by so fast.

I take another sip of my coffee and contemplate how freedom never felt so lonely. But I gaze down at my dog, Roy, who sits at my feet and looks up at me with his big brown eyes. He rises and nudges my arm as if to say: "It's going to be okay, Mom. Let's go for a walk."

88

WHERE IS IT?

I spoke to my daughter, Ashley, this morning. She's so excited because today is the day she is going to organize her laundry room and remove all things that don't belong, like old dog bowls and water glasses. My older daughter, Lindsay, is so proud of herself because she hired a person who specializes in organization and this gal made her baby closet go from looking like an explosion to a closet you could actually walk into.

This news delights me and makes me laugh. Both my daughters, as teenagers, had bedrooms that made me want to close their doors forever. Clothes were everywhere. But it was not as bad as my friend Jan's sister's bedroom. (I have changed the names to protect the innocent). Her sister, Lisa, had plates of "leftovers" under her bed, with stuff growing on them!

Being the daughter of a Marine, I had to keep my room super clean, while my parents gave up on my brothers' room, and simply closed the door. Some days, I really liked my neat room. Other days, I wished I could have made a mess, too, and gotten away with it, but my conscience would not let me.

Like my daughters, I can let messes get just so far, then I have to rein them in. "Mom, come look at my room now!" my daughters would say, individually, after they spent so many hours tidying up their rooms. I have to admit, I was relieved and happy for them. I didn't have to have a garage sale after all.

The hard part is making the time to get organized. This usually happens when I can't find something. And, it's never where you think you put it. I was looking for some name tags the other day for an event I was planning. I know I put them somewhere, but where? So, I took everything off the shelves in my office; took boxes out of my closet; tore the place apart but no name tags! So, I had to order new name tags, but in the process, I realized I had a lot of stuff that needed to go. I didn't need it anymore, so off to the shredder and trash can it went. I organized my office again and felt better, although "put out" because those darn name tags had disappeared into thin air!

Isn't that what our life is like? As hard as we try, we still clutter it with stuff we don't need, and don't declutter the stuff until we need to find something we really do need. But sometimes, it's worth the effort, because we can find a treasure in the mess.

I read about a family whose relatives found an actual live turtle in their attic the deceased had lost long ago. Apparently, the turtle survived on rain drops and bugs for years! And, some lady decided to finally pull all the weeds in her garden and in the process found a priceless ring she had lost, wrapped around a carrot! So, getting organized might be worth it. You never know what you might find.

PART VII

FINDING THE UPSIDE IN THE DOWNSIDES OF LIFE

89

LOVING ENOUGH TO SAY GOODBYE
TO MY OLD TREE
(NOVEMBER 2021)

I had to have my beautiful one-hundred-year-old Jacaranda tree cut down last week. One huge branch had slowly landed with a slight thump on my roof last year, thankfully causing zero damage. I tried to save her, taking off some of the heavy branches near some wires, but at last, I had to say goodbye to her.

Through tears I quietly thanked her for providing me with lovely purple blossoms in spring, and shade from her fern like leaves in summer. The tree is native to South America, so I have no clue why we have so many of these gorgeous ladies in California. But we are blessed, especially in the month of May, when you can drive down some streets and see many of them dancing in the breeze so proud of their purple blossoms.

I was reminded of the book, *The Giving Tree*, by Shel Silverstein, and how blessed we are to have trees and all the memories that come from them. When my brothers and I were children, we used to swing on vines from trees in the woods across the gully. Usually, we played all day in the woods with our friends, eating our sack lunches beneath the trees that our mothers made for us. My friend, Mary, and I often climbed the trees to spot box turtles. She, her sister, Judy, and I also made forts from fallen branches and leaves. An even earlier memory is being six years old, sitting beneath a giant elm tree with my childhood friend, Linda, as we had a picnic of white bread, blackberries, and pickles.

One Christmas, my father bought a small evergreen tree that we could decorate, but one we could plant after the holidays. We all participated in the planting of our tree by our driveway. It grew to be over a hundred feet tall, and as far as I know, it stands today, at our childhood home. Willow trees were the best, as they made great tents. Mary and I would play with our dolls for hours beneath the willow tree in my next-door neighbor's yard. Years later, I often sat beneath a giant oak tree at college to write my poetry. And, when I lived in New York City as a young professional writer, I will never forget walking through Central Park, sitting on a park bench, and reading, *A Tree Grows in Brooklyn*, by Betty Smith.

Trees give us so much joy and memories of times in our lives that I hope I never take them for granted. So, I planted a new Jacaranda tree in my front yard. She's only twenty feet tall and her branches are small. But, one day, when I am long gone, maybe someone else will hang a swing or hummingbird feeder on one of her branches. Maybe they will bask beneath her blossoms and fern like leaves and make new memories.

90

"JUST LOOK AT HOW FAR YOU'VE COME!"

(2024)

My cousin, Joe, is almost finished cleaning out his home to put it on the market. Due to some health issues, the process has taken him months. At times, he felt so discouraged. When we would speak on the phone every week or so, he would say: "I get so tired. I just can't do it!" And, I would keep telling him: "Just look at how far you've come!" I like to think that his being at the end of it all and the house now ready for market, that he will remember how far he has come.

For so many of us, life is one big tornado of self-doubt, fear of failure, worry about what other people will think or say or do, to bring us down and make us feel like one big pile of mush. I have been there, for sure.

When I was so proud of myself for finishing my first book, after months of hard work and being a full-time mother of two young daughters, I made the mistake of showing the galleys to my father, as I desperately wanted his approval. It was Christmas 1990, and my book was going to be published in the new year. But, my dad, whom I later learned had some issues, said to me: "Did you have all your marbles when you wrote this book?" If I could paint a visual, it felt like he had blown a big hole through my heart that day. It took me years of writing at my desk, struggling to continue my passion for writing, without crying.

Somehow, I felt like a failure. I felt like I was not enough, and would never be enough. I thought that no one would really care about my book, even though, in the new year, it was published, excerpted in three editions of *Reader's Digest* (USA, Great Britain, Canada), and I appeared on the *Today Show*, and many other programs. My book was also an alternate of the *Doubleday Book Club*, and I was interviewed by *USA Today*, the *Los Angeles Times*, and many publications around the country. My book, *How To Stay Lovers While Raising Your Children*, for married couples, was published not only in hardcover by *Price Stern Sloan*, but later in paperback by *St. Martin's Press*.

Years ago, when my two daughters, Ashley and Lindsay, my then husband, and I were all eating dinner at our favorite Chinese restaurant, a little hand reached up and tugged at my sleeve. With her sweet little face beaming, my then six-year-old daughter, Lindsay, looked up at me and said: "*I love your book, Mommy!*" And, it was then I realized how far I had come. I wrote a book. I took good care of my children. And the world did not crumble.

91

LISTEN TO A FIVE-YEAR-OLD
(MARCH 2023)

Everyone pretty much knows the story of *Beauty and the Beast*. It is a "tale as old as time." In fact, many versions of this story date back to the 1630's. But, told through the eyes of a five-year-old, one gains a new perspective on life. It was my joy a while back to *Facetime* with my granddaughter, Logan, at bedtime. After telling me every detail about her favorite doll's wardrobe and accessories, I asked her to read me a story from her favorite book.

She can only read a few words from her favorite story, *Beauty and the Beast*, so she smiles her cute smile and says: "I'm gonna read it *my way!*" "That's great!" I tell her. "You go right ahead." She begins to tell me the story, so excited, so animated, so wonderful. Her telling the story makes me feel like a child again. All my troubles and worries seem to melt away in the adorable sound of her voice.

To move her along, I kept saying, "And, then what happened?" and she would continue to tell me the story, and pause sometimes, to show me the pictures of Belle and the

Beast. As we moved along in the story, she tells me about the Beast who tries to save Belle from the wolves in the forest.

"And, the Beast saves Belle, but he gets injured," Logan explains. And, then she says: "The Beast's arm got hurt. But Belle fixed him up with *Duck Tape!*"

To say it was difficult not to roar with laughter at her excellent storytelling would be an understatement. Oh, I thought, how nice it would be to fix all our problems with *Duck Tape*. Then, I thought, what if we stopped worrying so much and could see life from the "up side," rather than the "down side."

It is easy to get sad or angry about a problem or situation, but I believe if we can ask God what He is trying to teach us through our trials, we would become stronger, and more able to help and comfort others. Not in every situation, of course, but most often, maybe all we need is a little *Duck Tape*. All our stories may not have happy endings, but we can have new beginnings.

92

PRAY, FIGHT, WIN!
(JULY 2023)

My beautiful daughter, Lindsay, turned forty years old recently. She and her husband, Shawn, spent several days in La Jolla, California, enjoying peaceful ocean waves, warm sunshine, and frolicking seals on the beach. I babysat my granddaughter, Brynn, and got four days of an amazing workout, like 40,000 steps and so many arm lifts I lost count. I got to play once again with this delightful toddler, who laughs even when I turn on the garbage disposal.

She is quite the character. She laughed as she danced in front of the huge bedroom mirror. She ate like a champ and slept like a dream. And, I was hugely grateful that all went well, because for one moment my daughter had the chance to forget the cruel "gift" she got turning forty, which was a "tumor" she discovered, along her left jawbone.

Thank God it is benign, but future surgery and recovery will be extreme and intense, and it breaks my heart. She is after all, my baby, my child, and I would rather it be me than her. But we are fighters in our family. Life has not always been kind, and at times, downright cruel. I am sure we are not the only family that has had to fight battles of many kinds, but how do we fight?

Most often we fight "on our knees," as they say. We pray a lot. Our friends pray a lot. We ask God to take these things away, but if not, then we ask God for the courage and strength to endure them, and please let everything turn out okay.

When my daughter was a toddler, I had to have a surgery and was not able to pick her up for weeks. But God brought amazing friends into my life who helped me. He does that, if we ask Him. God is our helper, our healer, our beloved counselor. It is unbearable at times, like the time I held my dying husband Michael's hand until it turned cold on a gray day in September of 2016. But I knew God was there because I felt His loving presence in the midst of my pain. In *2 Corinthians 1:4* in the Bible it reads: *He comforts us in all our troubles so that we can comfort others.*

Most days, I just want to be left alone. I do not bother life so why can't life leave us alone? My daughter works hard. She is a devoted mother. She doesn't deserve this "thing." She takes excellent care of herself, so why? Only God knows and He is not telling me right now. So, we pray. We fight. And we will win!

93

WE NEED TO MAKE MOLE HILLS OUT OF MOUNTAINS

(2024)

My old car needs another repair. My old cat is losing weight. And my oldest daughter needs another surgery on her jaw. These are not easy situations. They make me sad and want to crawl back into bed. But I am grateful that my daughter can get her jaw straightened and she will smile again. I am thankful my twenty-year-old cat is still around and is my good buddy. And, getting my car fixed, well, I am hopeful it will last a few more years.

I was reminded this morning of that old saying: "Don't make a mountain out of a mole hill." Where did it come from and what does it mean? The expression is more than 350 years old, having come from a book by James Howell in 1660. It means that we are not supposed to make our problems bigger than they are.

Another phrase is: "Don't make an elephant out of a fly!" For example, if your ice cream fell off your ice cream cone onto the floor, as mine did when I was nine years old, you should not cry or throw a hissy fit. It is just ice cream, and the lady gave me a new ice cream cone after my mom dried my tears.

In other words, check yourself if you are over reacting. If you can, take moles out of the mountain. Do not take on the whole mountain. Take some baby steps until the problem is resolved. Breathe.

When I was very young, I used to avoid conflict, thinking my life would be simple. Don't anyone dare bother me, I thought. I am just going to live in a cabin in the woods like Henry David Thoreau and forget about the world. But the world finds you eventually. Trials, conflicts, and annoyances are unavoidable.

Problems creep into our lives like ants under our windowsills. As difficult as it is, I try to look at the upside of these irritating "moles" before they turn into the "mountains" I have no interest in climbing.

Trials build character we are told. As a wife who took care of her husband who had ALS until he died, yes, I know about trials. As a mom who watched her daughter being wheeled away for a six-hour surgery, I am familiar with situations that make you want to cry your eyes out. But I have learned that life goes on. Situations can get better. And, so I am still learning to take baby steps every day. Those moles that are trying to become mountains in my life I have learned I can manage, because I have managed them before. And just maybe we can even learn to be grateful for those moles, because if we let them, they can offer us mountains of strength.

94

INCONVENIENCES CAN ACTUALLY
BE BLESSINGS

"An inconvenience is an unrecognized opportunity," said Confucius once, no doubt experiencing one. Oh, we all gripe and complain, but if you think about it, maybe being delayed in traffic caused you to miss an accident on the freeway that day, or maybe that plane malfunction kept you safe, as well.

When my family and I lived in San Rafael, California, years ago, I often took my two daughters on a ferry boat ride from Larkspur Landing into Embarcadero, in San Francisco. We would ride on the carousel and go to the various shops on Pier 39. The one day we could not go and stayed home, was when the 1989 Loma Prieta earthquake hit on October 17th. We marked ourselves "safe" at home, after our house went up and then down, as if a huge animal went underneath us. Thankfully, no damage had occurred.

In July 1996, our family attended The Summer Olympics in Atlanta. We had a wonderful day watching the women's diving event, eating in some fun restaurants, and shopping for Olympic pins to put on the hats we wore. It was a Friday evening, July 26th, when we decided to take the train back to the home of our friends where we were staying. My daughters put up a fuss, as they longed to stay later. But, our decision to leave proved to be a smart one, as we were hanging around Centennial Olympic Park. Early Saturday morning, at 1:20 am, on July 27th, a domestic terrorist pipe bombing attack occurred, killing one person, and injuring 111 others.

On Saturday, August 13th, 2005, the baggage handlers' strike occurred at Heathrow Airport, in London, as we were sitting on a plane headed for Paris. We sat on the tarmac for four hours, then had to get off the plane with no luggage. I think the words of my daughters' dad were music to their ears when he said: "You have to shop!" As he checked us into a London hotel, my daughters and I frantically ran up the street to a local boutique and shopped for clothes and supplies. The manager and clerks were so thoughtful, and kept the store open for an extra twenty minutes at closing time. A couple days later, we took the Chunnel (the Channal Tunnel) to Paris and ended up having a great vacation, despite not getting our luggage back until two weeks after we returned home.

In December of 2022, I went to visit my youngest daughter, Ashley, and family for Christmas in Wisconsin. Due to winter storms, my older daughter, Lindsay, and family had their flight canceled and did not arrive until the day *after* Christmas.

My flight got canceled several times as I tried to return home before New Year's Eve. As it turned out, we *all* got to be together for New Year's Eve, which was so wonderful. We had fun playing board games by a crackling fire, and cooking up amazing meals, while the wind chill factor outside got down to eleven degrees below zero.

Sometimes, life does not turn out as planned. As Renee Zellweger said in one of my all-time favorite movies, *New in Town*, "…Nothing about Minnesota is what I planned." And, sometimes, we learn, as cultural historian, Siva Vaidhyanathan once said: "It turns out inconvenience was a really important part of our lives, and we didn't even realize it."

95

WHY CELEBRATIONS OF LIFE ARE IMPORTANT
(APRIL 2023)

I was blessed to attend two celebrations within a few days of each other, a celebration of life, for the passing of a dear friend's husband into Heaven; and a dear friend's 70th birthday party, attended also by her mother who is 104! Both celebrations were memorable.

My friends and I were sad to see our dear friend, Bill, change addresses on us and go to Heaven. We miss him, especially his wife, my dear friend, Yvonne. In the middle of eulogies, the slides of our friend's life, the flowers, the food, and conversations, we realized that we were sad to not hear him laugh and tell his jokes anymore. Everyone loved Bill. And he adored Yvonne. Bill was a "Buckeye," who attended Ohio State University. How he loved his "Buckeyes!" We always joked with each other, as I am a Buckeye, too, having grown up in Ohio.

Bill was dear friends with Judy, the birthday girl, and Judy's husband, Al. Yvonne sat next to me at Judy's party. There were several guests. We sat outside on a gorgeous

Sunday, at a table on this beautiful patio surrounded by tropical plants, ate Mexican food, laughed, and sang, "Happy Birthday," to Judy. I could imagine Bill looking down at us from lofty white clouds, his eternal home, and smiling.

Though we are sad Bill is no longer with us, we celebrated "life," because we were grateful for so many things, our times together as friends, our times together with family members, and for all the memories. Each day is a gift and a reason to celebrate. Though we have heard this message so many times before, when we open each day with gratitude, God gives us presents.

96

ONE MYSTERIOUS NIGHT

M any of us have heard the saying, "God works in mysterious ways," and that sometimes, as it says in the Bible (Hebrews 13:2): *Do not forget to entertain strangers, for by so doing some have unwittingly entertained angels.* There was only one other time, besides this one evening I will tell you about, that I believe my two daughters and I were possibly visited by an angel.

It was summer. My daughter, Lindsay, was eight-and-a-half years old, and Ashley was six years old. I took them to our local library. We were standing on the steps of the library and realized that it was closed, when suddenly, out of nowhere, a man came up to us with a huge, leather-bound Bible in his hands. "Would you like to have this?" he asked us. "Okay," I answered, and in a flash he was gone. "Mommy!" my daughter Ashley suddenly cried out. "That was an angel!"

This event was many years ago, and the memory of it still fills me with curiosity and wonder. My daughter's reaction and her words were totally spontaneous. We had not even talked about angels in a long time that I could recall.

More recently, I had been a caregiver for my husband, Michael, who was dying from ALS. In a matter of three short years, he had gone from having pain behind his right knee, to having to use a cane, then a walker, then a scooter, which was becoming difficult for him to manage. His voice had become a whisper. In February 2016, he had lost the use of his legs.

Through the help of hospice nurses, I had learned how to use a strap under his armpits to help lift him from the bed to his scooter, from his scooter to the toilet, off the toilet to his scooter, to his chair at our kitchen table, off the chair to the scooter and to his recliner. In the evening it was reversed. Sometimes, he wanted to attend the church of his best friend about forty minutes from where we lived. I would put him on his scooter and guide him out to our car. Then I would gently lift him off the scooter into the passenger side seat, then out of the passenger side seat onto his scooter to go into the church.

Sometimes, the men at this church would help me lift Michael into the pew and so on. The scooter was a smaller collapsible one, but it weighed seventy pounds. I had an old hatchback car, so I would lift the front end of the scooter onto the back of my car, then lift the back end of the scooter and slide it into my car. Sometimes, I would lift all seventy pounds of the scooter and place it into my car.

And, lifting Michael was another story. One day, I counted that I lifted my husband sixteen times! The incredibly difficult and heart wrenching work of caring for my husband often found me on my knees asking God for strength to keep going. And, I had no idea how long I could keep going, so every day I just kept praying, "God, give me strength for today."

By June 2016, it was becoming much harder for me to lift Michael. He was six feet tall, and had been losing weight, but at my height of five-foot-four, it was a struggle. I still do not know how I did it, although I would rise very early in the morning, when Michael could still manage, and work out with a trainer at my local gym, lifting weights as a matter of survival.

One evening in June 2016, I could not lift my husband out of his recliner, as hard as I tried. It was three days before I had to put him into an assisted living facility with hospice care because, after five months and him losing most of his strength, my strength was fading, too. It was a sad and difficult decision for both of us, as he still had clarity of mind.

In desperation, I called our local fire department, told them my situation, and asked for help. A fire truck, lights flashing but no siren, pulled up in front of our home. Out jumped four, six-foot-four young firemen who came to my front door. I let them in and they greeted me very kindly. I could sense a loving strength from them and it helped me to totally relax. Then, very gently, with two of them on each side of Michael, they lifted him up and laid him gently in our bed. They came two more nights after that to help me. On the last night, I thanked them profusely as they left. I closed the front door, walked into our bedroom, gazed at Michael sleeping soundly in our bed, and thought, but God...

97

IT'S GONNA BE OKAY (IGBOK)

O nce upon a time, there was an *ABC* television series, *Nashville*, a country musical drama created by Callie Khouri, of *Thelma and Louise* movie fame. The show was a remarkable success, produced by Dee Johnson, Khouri, Steve Buchanan and Connie Britton.

It starred Britton, Hayden Panettiere, Clare Bowen, Eric Close, Charles Eaten, Jonathan Jackson, Sam Palladio, Judith Hoag, and many others. The series starred Britton as Rayna Jaymes, a fading country music superstar, pitted against rising country star, Julliette Barnes, portrayed by Panettiere.

My daughter, Lindsay, had the privilege of being one of the producers during the first season, which began October 10, 2012. When I went to Nashville to visit her and shadow the cast and crew, we had so much fun. While my daughter worked hard, I got to sit in a director's chair and observe. The glitz of being on the set was exciting, but it was just enjoyable being in this amazing city. We went to the Bluebird Café, The Grand Ole Opry House and saw Carrie

Underwood, and to Leiper's Fork where we listened to a little country band in a small grocery store with a wooden floor.

Later, we went to this art gallery where a pure white American Pit Bull Terrier stood guard at the door, who just wanted to be friends. It was there I saw something I wanted. It was not much, but it caught my eye. There amongst the paintings on the walls and the hand painted greeting cards, I saw a black bumper sticker with white letters spelling "igbok" (It's gonna be okay).

Little did I know how important this message was going to be for my daughter and me. After a highly successful first season, and my daughter's anticipated move to a permanent home in Nashville seemed imminent, a new producer was hired who brought in a whole new crew. The old crew was out. My daughter was devastated, but had to accept the fact that this was "show business."

I tend to think that things happen for a reason. While I was sad for my daughter, the years going forward brought many blessings. I got to have some family nearby, rather than having both my daughters living in other states. My daughter found other jobs over the years, a devoted husband, and started her family. What I have learned is that things can change in an instant. We need to appreciate each new day that brings new experiences, opportunities, and people. Sometimes, the grass *can* be greener on the other side, even if we must step on the grass over the septic tank to get there!

98

WHAT THE FIRES CAN'T TAKE AWAY FROM US

(JANUARY 2025)

"Mom, the fires are getting close and we need to evacuate; do you still have the *Pack 'N Play*?" asked my daughter, Lindsay. The horrific California fires in the Pacific Palisades, Altadena, and the Greater Los Angeles area were raging. As my daughter, her husband, Shawn, and daughter, Brynn, were packing up to come south to where I live, I could hear the almost panic in her voice.

When they arrived at my house, they filled it up with their suitcases, toys, special foods and their need for comfort and love. I babysat my granddaughter while they both tried to work and think, but we were all on edge. As we checked on the news from time to time, my granddaughter filled my home with her light and laughter. I was glad for her innocence and no awareness of what we were dealing with.

We played in my backyard, as the smoke had not reached my area. We played, "let's give baby doll a bath," "let's build a fort out of blankets," "let's have a picnic." Later, my daughter and I took her to this beautiful park where she enjoyed climbing on the jungle gym, going down the slide and making new friends. A friend of mine took us out to dinner that night at a local fun restaurant to ease our anxiety. It helped briefly.

But it was getting dicey by the time we put Brynn to sleep in my guest room. The fires were now approaching the Hollywood Bowl and the Hollywood Sign. Needless-to-say, none of us got much sleep, as we were all worried and wondering if my daughter and son-in-law would have a home to go home to. We prayed and many of our friends prayed and texted us to see if we were safe.

We found out the next morning that these fires near their home had been put out and their place was safe. But we wept for those who had lost their homes. In the surreal atmosphere of trying to wrap our heads around these fires and the enormous destruction of so many homes, my granddaughter is coloring in her coloring book and watching her favorite television show.

My daughter and I took a short walk to my local country grocery store, bought sandwiches, and talked to the owners there. How I appreciated their friendly faces and words of comfort that day. How I appreciated the fact that my daughter, son-in-law, and granddaughter were safe in my home. At least "we have each other," I kept telling myself.

In the aftermath of the fires, we learned, to date, that thirty people died, 57,665 acres were burned, and 16,255 structures were destroyed. It is a tragedy that will not long be forgotten, as residents rebuild or leave the area forever. A few days later, when it was safe for my daughter, son-in-law, and granddaughter to return to their home that was still standing, I hugged them goodbye. And I thought to myself, while we weep for the unfathomable losses, nothing can take away, love.

Hundreds of volunteers helped get supplies to families in need. Hundreds of people provided shelters, and prayers and comfort, because hundreds were not going to let the fires win.

99

WHAT WE CAN LEARN FROM CLOSE CALLS

I t's the "call" no one wants to get. I had just arrived in Wisconsin to visit my youngest daughter, Ashley, when my youngest brother, John, called, regarding our brother, Dan. "He's been in a car accident," John said, when we talked late in the evening. "He was driving home, fell asleep at the wheel and hit a tree."

There was the mention of a brain bleed, broken ribs, at the hospital, does not remember anything. I went into hyper prayer mode. I texted every prayer warrior friend I knew, prayer teams from my church and another church, and several women's prayer teams. Awake most of the night waiting for more news, I prayed that my brother would live, that he would be okay.

After surgery to fuse seven vertebrae, a tube put into his lungs to drain fluid, and news that any brain bleed was minor and no longer an issue, I could breathe again. When I finally got a text from Dan I cried. And, when he was moved out of intensive care to the trauma center and later to a reha-

266

bilitation facility, I thanked God for answered prayer. But what really got to me was a song Dan texted to me. It was *Fires*, by Jordan St. Cyr. Some of the lyrics go like this:

> *(chorus)*
> You've walked me through fires
> Pulled me from flames
> If You're in this with me
> I won't be afraid
> When the smoke billows higher, oh and
> higher
> And it feels like I can barely breathe
> I'll walk through these fires
> Cause You're walking with me...

How often have we all been pulled from the flames in our lives? When I was an editor in New York City, a construction crane just missed hitting a lady on the sidewalk when it fell. My youngest daughter survived with minor bruises in a road rage incident when the guy driver of the other car wouldn't let her exit and she spun around and hit a wall. My former brother-in-law was late for work, gets a call from a friend telling him to not take the train into Manhattan because a plane had just hit the World Trade Center. And, the list goes on and on.

If I am delayed from getting on the freeway, or if my plane is delayed due to mechanical problems, I am grateful. No one wants a close call. None of us wants to be inconvenienced, but maybe these events are blessings in disguise, or "wake up calls." I used to get upset. Now, I try to learn something from them. Yes, we need to be careful. My brother maybe should have not burned the candle at both ends. He maybe should have pulled over and gotten a cup of coffee on his way home. Maybe we should all listen to that "feeling" when something does not feel right. God is warning us of something.

Sometimes, things are unavoidable. I didn't count on that drunk driver killing my boyfriend as he walked along the side of the road at a Christian youth conference. Sometimes, we don't see things coming. But I do believe in so many ways that God protects us, tries to get us to listen. I'll just say it, life sucks sometimes. But, when we shake off the lightening bolts of what almost hit us, maybe we gain some clarity.

PART VIII

GROWING FORWARD

100

TRANSITIONS ARE NEVER EASY

(2024)

My daughter, Lindsay, called me the other day. It was her daughter, Brynn's second week at preschool. Instead of staying with her the three whole hours, my daughter decided to drop her off and see how she would do. I could hear her crying over the phone. It was not my granddaughter who was crying, but my daughter. "She said, 'Bye mama,' and went off to play," Lindsay related. It was a bittersweet moment.

Seeing our kids go through their own transitions certainly affects ours. As parents, we bid goodbye to our children who have suddenly become college freshman and off on their own. This transition is especially difficult. I still remember the mornings my daughters, Lindsay and Ashley, at separate times, coming down the stairs on the day we were to fly clear across the country from Texas to California to get them settled into college.

I still remember thinking, this is the last morning of my

daughters being home with us as our children in this way. This is the last time they will be my little girls before they go off on their own, being their own persons, living their own lives. It was so abrupt it seemed, that I could not even comprehend it.

The times of our lives go by so fast. One minute we are changing diapers as sleep deprived moms of newborns, then we are taxi drivers for all our kids' activities, then we hold our breath and say a prayer as they drive off solo with their new driver's license. We race through life so fast trying to keep up that we can only capture it in pictures or videos, or in my favorite way, in the sixty plus diaries I have stuffed in boxes in my closet.

I still remember our first cross country flight. My daughter, Lindsay, slept on my lap as I stroked her hair and gazed down at the mountains and terrain below. I remember thinking that this would be the last time I would stroke her hair like this, the last time she would sleep on my lap.

With my second daughter, Ashley, I remember staring at her little body through the maternity ward nursery window, thinking this would be the last time I would give birth to another precious child, and I wanted to savor every minute with her. I mentally tried to capture her sweet baby sounds, and even recorded her and my other daughter on my old tape recorder.

With Ashley, I remember her newborn frog legs kept getting longer and longer and then she learned to walk one Christmas when she was nine months old. I have a cute video of her toddling to Raffi's song, *Old Toy Train*. It seemed that no matter how hard I tried to grasp each moment of my daughters' lives, time just didn't "march on;" it flew by so fast

I was not even aware of it. Then, one day, they were all grown up with children of their own. How could this happen I often wonder, when I still feel so young inside?

But the good news is that time gives us a little more time to savor more "firsts." And this is the most precious gift of all.

101

WHAT WE CAN LEARN FROM DEFEAT
(OCTOBER 2024)

Recently, my daughter, Ashley, and son-in-law Jeff's favorite baseball team, the Milwaukee Brewers, suffered a crushing defeat, in what seemed to be a sure bet heading to Philadelphia in the National League Division. It was so close that their bags were packed to go to Philadelphia, as Jeff is a broadcaster for the Brewers. Then, in a split second, it was all over for the season.

"Everyone was crying," said my daughter. "It was hard to take." It was especially devastating because it was Bob Uecker's last season as a broadcaster for the Brewers and they all wanted to "win it" for him. I'm sure all of us can remember feeling defeated at some point in our lives. At first, we are in shock, then we are so disappointed, then, as we try to wrap our heads around this big dark ball of heartbreak, we try to tell ourselves we will be okay.

But it takes a while, as we try to analyze what went wrong, what we could have done better, and what the heck just happened! How do we move on when we don't even feel like getting out of bed? How do we begin to believe that good things in our future will ever be possible?

But one day someone encourages us. One day we get a break. One day something wonderful can and does happen if we just hang in there. I have a plaque in my kitchen with a quote by Theodore Roosevelt that reads: "Believe you can, and you're halfway there." For it is in the believing that "we can" that starts the engine to accomplishing our goals, and seeing the "light" at the end of the tunnel. Thomas Edison, after 10,000 failures, invented electricity. The Wright brothers, Orville and Wilbur, endured hunger, bitter cold and many defeats, until one day, they successfully flew their fragile plane at Kitty Hawk, South Carolina.

And, Helen Keller, rose above her many handicaps and trials with the help of Anne Sullivan, her instructor and friend, to become an inspiration for many people.

What is defeat anyway, when you pick yourself up out of the mud, brush yourself off, find that inspiration again, and step back on to the road to success? Trudge on, dear ones, trudge on. As the poet, Robert Browning, once said: "Grow old along with me! The best is yet to be..." Each defeat makes us wiser with age. It is in our growing older and wiser where we can see our mistakes as lessons, our trials as stepping stones, and our defeats as ways to pick ourselves up, bolster our courage, and keep growing forward.

102

THE BASEBALL LIFE OF A BASEBALL WIFE

"Jeff leaves on Wednesday," my daughter Ashley tells me. I could sense the sadness in her voice, yet stoic determination as their eleventh baseball season with the Milwaukee Brewers was about to begin with Spring training in Arizona. My son-in-law, Jeff, is a sports broadcaster for the Milwaukee Brewers. They are proud and grateful for Jeff's opportunities, but like the pioneer wife, my daughter must keep the home fires burning and their two kids growing, mostly by herself.

During Spring training, my daughter and her husband are apart for a month. "Before my oldest kid started kindergarten, we would stay the whole month of Spring training with my husband," Ashley explains. "But once my kids were in school, we could no longer do this."

During baseball season Jeff is mostly away from February until October, with times at home when the Brewers play home games at American Family Field. Sometimes Ashley and their two kids will fly to whatever city Jeff is in to see a game or two in the summer. It is not an easy life, and reminds me of the ever supportive and encouraging wife, Lorri Morris, played by actress, Rachel Griffiths, in the true story movie, *The Rookie*. She tells her husband, Jim Morris, played by Dennis Quaid, who obtains the opportunity of a lifetime to play for the Tampa Bay Devil Rays: "Jimmy Morris, I'm a Texas woman, which means I don't need the help of a man to keep things runnin!" My strong daughter spent nine years of her life growing up in Texas, but there have been times when life has been hard holding down the fort at their home in Wisconsin.

"One of the worst times was when I flew by myself to Texas for a friend's bridal shower with my young son and baby daughter," remembers Ashley. "Coming home I got sick, and trying to take care of two kids by myself, flying on the plane from Dallas to Milwaukee and being so ill was difficult." To date, my daughter has flown to many cities where the Brewers were playing, and to visits with family members around the country by herself with the kids. She has learned a lot and gained so much strength.

My daughter has always been good eliciting the help of neighbors along the way, but just like most wives whose husbands might be in the military or who travel all the time, life can be challenging going it alone. Making sure the kids are well fed, do well in school, dealing with home repairs and a million other details of life alone while husbands are away, is something most wives "should be acknowledged" for. I know what it is like, as I was one of them. So, here's to all the wives and mothers who "hold down the fort" in so many ways on so many days during a year. Pat yourselves on the back for all the growing you do, especially during the tough times.

103

BEING MY OWN PERSON

What is it about life that is most difficult? I would have to say, communication. Since the perfect family is rare, we learn how to communicate through our family of origin. If it was good communication, then we are set. If it was not, we either learned new tools or failed in old habits we refuse to give up. But since we all are a "work in progress," I suspect we have been learning how to communicate for a very long time now.

It is much harder today and I won't go into all that. What I want to talk about are "communication tools," in a class I am taking. There are about fifteen of us. We meet in my girlfriend's home, go over work sheets and talk about our lives. We learn on the work sheets, for example, what is the "best option," in various communication situations.

Last night's discussion had to do with control issues. Are you a "controller," or "out of control?" In other words, do you try to control others because you feel insecure, or do you allow others to control you because you are a "people pleaser," and afraid to speak up, afraid of conflict? So, what is the middle ground? It is being able to "control yourself."

Self-control is the best option here. If you try to control your spouse or partner, which is just an illusion, you bring about what you fear, possibly an angry spouse or partner, or one who might just withdraw. If you are allowing yourself to be controlled, you will not be a happy camper. In the long run it does not help your relationship or you as an individual.

As for myself, I had been a "people pleaser" for a long time, thinking the more I gave, the more I would get back. But it does not work out that way. The more I gave the more unhappy I became. I learned there are the "takers," and there are the "givers" in this world. And, the "takers" will just keep on taking. I felt, at one point, that I was losing myself.

Being in control of oneself is a full-time job, but I have to say I'm the happiest I have been in years. I take care of myself. Life has not been easy, but it is what you make it. I am in control of "me!" And it is a great relief to realize that I do not have to take care of anyone. They can take care of themselves and I can just take care of me. A mother must take care of her young children, of course, but I'm talking about adults here.

I can love my family members. I can offer advice when asked. I can detach, too, and be proud of the lives my loved ones are living. Once my husband Michael told me he thought his mother was "the amoeba of love." And, one young lady in our communications group cried as she told us about her twin sister who still controls every aspect of her life, even though she has a husband who loves her deeply.

To the controllers out there, all I can say is the quote

from Viola Davis's character, Aibileen Clark, to Bryce Dallas Howard's character, Hilly, in the movie, *The Help*: "Ain't you tired?" And to the controlled: "Ain't you tired?" I'd just rather be my own person, healthy boundaries in place, responsibilities for self, in charge of me, my person.

104

SOMETIMES YOU JUST HAVE TO DANCE!

One day, when my granddaughter, Brynn, was two years old, my daughter, Lindsay, and I took her to a music class. The studio was decorated in "lady bugs" with cute lady bug rugs, which we sat on. There were about ten adorable two-year-olds all sitting on their mothers' laps.

The teacher came out with her guitar and started singing such kids' songs as, *If You're Happy and You Know It Clap Your Hands*, and *Bingo*. Immediately, my granddaughter gets up and starts dancing. I get up and start dancing with her. Pretty soon, other kids and moms, everyone was dancing with assorted scarves, tambourines, Maracas! It was a total blast. I had forgotten how much "fun" being a "kid" was.

One Friday night, two girlfriends and I went to listen to a friend's band and hear her sing at a place called Lone Wolf Brewery. Our friend, Diana Drake, who used to open for many famous artists in Las Vegas, belted out such familiar songs like Tina Turner's *Proud Mary*, and Nancy Sinatra's *These Boots Are Made For Walkin'*. We, of course, had to get on the dance floor and dance with lots of other people. I forgot how much fun it was to be a "teenager" again.

On Saturday night, several of my friends and I went to a restaurant and watched some amazing couples dance to *Cotton-Eyed Joe*, and *Swimming Upstream*, with dance moves such as the "Pretzel." We tried some line dancing and had so much fun. How I lived in Texas for fourteen years and did not learn the "Electric Slide," is beyond me. Oh, wait a minute! I was a taxi driver for my two adolescents then. Well, on the recent dance night, it sure felt good to feel forty again!

So, whether you go to a music class, or to a restaurant with a great band and dance floor, or just have a dance party in your living room, get out there and dance your legs off! Move whatever moves. Shake, but not too much, whatever still shakes. Dancing to great music is the "real" fountain of youth, and we are not done yet!

105

WHAT BUTTERFLIES CAN TEACH US

My friend, Cecelia, has forty-four monarch butterflies in chrysalis forms ready to emerge into the world. She has been attracting these butterflies for years now with her milkweed plants. She protects the eggs, nurtures the caterpillars, and watches like a mother hen over a special butterfly habitat until the new butterflies emerge from their cocoons, dry their wings, and fly away.

By mid-August the monarch butterflies, with their black-veined, orange-paneled wings then begin their migration from Canada and the United States, to Mexico, as they travel 3,000 miles on their journey. For any of us needing a break from our "troubled world," we can immerse ourselves in the wonders of nature. It is then, we can begin anew, like the butterfly.

Most of us know what it is like to dive into a cool lake or ocean or swimming pool. Under the water there is a quiet, a sense of calm and joy. And most of us know what it is like to walk along a path in the quiet woods beneath a canopy of green trees tossing their branches in the wind. The time is now to give yourself permission to be a child again, to rest your weary souls in places of comfort and peace. Nature can do that.

When was the last time you went on a picnic, laid on a blanket and looked up at the sky? Or watched a total sunset melt into the purple clouds at dusk? Or sat by a campfire and looked up and counted the stars? It is okay to just "be."

Like the busy monarch caterpillar, it is okay to wrap ourselves in our own chrysalis form, to shed our worries and fears in a place of rest. In doing so, we give ourselves a chance to rise refreshed, and ready to fly again, no matter where our journeys may take us.

106

SLOANE, OUR MIRACLE BABY

In July 2023, my oldest daughter, Lindsay, who was about to celebrate her 40th birthday, wanted to have child number two. Instead, she got hit with news she never expected. Her chiropractor noticed the left side of her jaw looked larger than the right side. A good neighbor of hers, an ear, nose, and throat specialist, encouraged her to get a CT scan, which revealed a tumor in her jaw. Thank goodness it turned out to be benign, but with a deep sadness, she jokingly remarked: "Instead of having a baby I got a tumor!"

She had to have two intense surgeries, one that lasted six hours and another surgery six months later that lasted four hours, followed by many more months of recovery and doctor visits. She had long given up trying for baby number two.

But then a miracle happened. In fact, when she realized she was pregnant again and went to see her gynecologist he said to her: "Miracles happen every day!" So, we are waiting with bated breath for the blessed event, another little girl.

My three-year-old granddaughter is so excited she is going to have a baby sister, although I'm not sure she knows what all this entails. "Our baby is a cabbage!" she proudly announces, regarding the current size of her baby sister.

"I'm going to have a baby sister and I'm going to change her poopy diapers," Brynn adds. I pray these two sisters will be close always, as my two daughters are. A day does not go by where Lindsay and Ashley do not talk to each other, and miss each other, living many miles apart. I pray they will always encourage one another, support one another, love one another, as two sisters can. It is a blessing to have a sibling, and I count myself doubly blessed with my two brothers in my life.

In God's Word we read: "*...For You formed my inward parts; you covered me in my mother's womb. I will praise You, for I am fearfully and wonderfully made... Psalm 139: 13-14...*

God is certainly a miracle worker, preserving my own daughter, Lindsay, after her tumor scare and surgeries, to have her second daughter, Sloane. Because miracles "do happen" every day.

107

WALKING OUT WHERE THE SOUL
CAN BREATHE

When Emma Gatewood (known as Grandma Gatewood) was sixty-seven years old, she told her three grown children still living at home (she had eleven children total) that she was going for a walk. This was on May 3, 1955. She had worked the family farm in Gallia County, Ohio, for years, and endured frequent physical abuse at the hand of her husband (later divorced him), so her children knew she was "one strong woman."

She could handle anything, certainly another walk in the woods, her place of sanctuary. A few days prior, she had read an article in *National Geographic*, about the Appalachian Trail (A.T.). She decided to walk the length of it, from Georgia to Maine, which was over 2,000 miles, with just a shower curtain to protect herself from the rain, her *Keds* sneakers, and a knapsack of provisions.

Strangers were kind in those days, and as news began to spread about her walk, they gave her food, shelter, and clothing along her route. When articles were published in newspapers about her, that is when her kids found out what she was up to, and they felt proud of their mother. She finally made it to the top of Mount Katahdin in Maine, on September 25, 1955, after 146 days of walking, and going through fifteen pairs of *Keds*. She became a legend.

The next year, she walked the A.T. again, and then hiked several more places. She appeared on national television programs and did much to make sure the A.T. was updated and clearly marked for future hikers. She became a life member of the National Campers and Hikers Association and the Roanoke Appalachian Trail Club. When she was in her eighties, she spent many hours a day clearing and marking a 30-mile hiking trail through Gallia County that was connected to the Buckeye Trail.

And, in 1973, just prior to her death, she took an open-ended bus trip all around the United States and parts of Canada. By the time she made her last "spiritual hike" to Heaven, passing away on June 4, 1973, she had logged in more than 14,000 miles, equal to more than halfway around the world!

It was upon reading about her first hike to the top of Mount Katahdin in the book, *Grandma Gatewood's Walk* (*Chicago Review Press*, 2014) by Ben Montgomery, that struck me the most. When she reached the top of the mountain, she stopped for a moment to catch her breath. She gazed all around her at the sky and the trees below. She felt the cool breeze on her cheeks, and sang the song, *America the Beautiful*. When she finished singing, she then said: "I *did* it!"

There is a tremendous feeling of satisfaction when you reach the top of a challenging hill or mountain, and look out at the beautiful places God has gifted us. I know hiking is not for everyone, but nature is. Even if you go out to the woods and sit on a rock, or fish in a pristine lake, or watch an amazing sunrise over a mountaintop, there is something incredible about being out where our souls can breathe. In our hurried calamitous world, we all need nature more than we know. It is why God gave it to us, even if all we can say is: "I *see* it!

108

ONE DAY ON THE ROGUE RIVER

This one is for the books because I am often hesitant about trying anything new. I usually must force myself to try new things and overthink everything. I feel anxiety even when I am doing something fun, as I try to talk myself into being brave. So here is my story, me being brave, which to this day I can hardly believe we did this...

"I've been river rafting before," said our friend, Sally, so yeah, Judy and I figured she knew what she was doing. Sally drove us to a well-equipped qualified company that rented rafts for trips down the Rogue River, near Medford, Oregon. Once avid hikers all of us, Judy and I knew very little about river rafting, but we decided to give it a try with Sally as our guide. This adventure was a few years ago, in July.

We got our stuff together, life jackets, paddles, and other gear like a picnic basket and water bottles, sunscreen, hats, and we were ready to go. A guy driving a bus took us to the place where we picked up our raft to go on "class 2" rapids, which at first, seemed tame. Being the strongest one of our group I took a deep breath and thought, what could go wrong? This will be fun! Sally knew the various strokes. She would instruct us.

Some guy with the river raft company helped us get into our raft, get our paddles ready and away we went. The way we were positioned it was Sally in front, Judy in the middle and me in the back of our raft. It was so peaceful at first, calm, just going down the river on a sunny day. The guy explained where we needed to get off down the river, the drop off point, which was quite a few miles away. This is so much fun we all thought. I always wanted to play, "Huckleberry Finn," I'm thinking, how cool is this? And, later, we will just paddle over to the river bank and have our picnic.

Well, when we decided to "shoot the rapids" it was like nothing I had ever experienced before. The rapids were much swifter than I expected and we had to maneuver around some rocks. The adrenaline rush was something I only experienced on a smaller scale on a roller coaster when I was a kid. Somehow, I knew that you had to paddle "hard" into the direction of the rapids, which I did, and instructed Sally and Judy to do the same. So, we did okay and it was a wild fun ride. We experienced exhilarating relief after conquering the rapids as we floated into the calm part of the river, then there were more rapids and more rapids.

At one point, Sally decided she wanted to steer. Suddenly, we started going round and round and round, like "three men in a tub." I took over, using all my muscles to steer us towards the river bank so we could have our picnic. We all paddled hard. As we neared the river bank a tree branch almost hit Sally in the face. She grabbed it, but in doing so, fell backwards right into Judy's crotch! We all started laughing hysterically as a surprised Judy exclaimed: "I feel like I'm birthing!"

After laughing our faces off, we found a calm area beneath a sloping tree and had our lunch. Wow, this is the life I thought. How brave are we? Or maybe stupid, but we had so much fun. The hard part, however, was just ahead of us.

As we paddled out into the river again, we were hit with a steeper gradient and more wild rapids. With the spray hitting our faces and adrenaline pumping, we once again felt like we were on some incredible roller coaster ride. Please God, I'm praying silently, do not let us tip over like the couple on the raft we just passed in a flash. The river in most places was only three feet deep but the current was very swift.

We made it through the rapids and could relax in the calm parts. Floating down the river in the warm sunshine made us feel like young women again, strong women, maybe even a bit like pioneer women. And we were proud of ourselves.

Pretty soon our drop off point was approaching, as were more rapids. If we missed it, who knew where we would end up? If we went passed it, we would have to carry our huge raft back to the drop off point so the company bus guy could pick us up.

As Sally was trying to steer, I took command again and told Judy: "Paddle, Judy! Paddle *hard*! We can't miss our drop off point!" With all the strength we could muster, in the middle of the rapids, we paddled like our lives depended on it. And, we finally managed to get our raft over to the river bank at last!

Judy and Sally were so tired and done with our adventure that they immediately climbed out of the raft and fell into the shallow water. I was exhausted too, in a good way, but I saw a guy about to launch his kayak on the ramp into the river so I waited. He looked at me and I looked at him. He smiled, grabbed the rope on the raft and pulled me onto the ramp. "I see you're the smart one," he said with a laugh. I smiled, stepped out of the raft onto dry land and we helped Judy and Sally get out of the water.

All-in-all it was the adventure of a lifetime that I will always remember with my girlfriends. After we got back home to Sally's house, I couldn't help but ask her: "I thought you said you went river rafting before?" "Oh, yes," she said. "That was with a guide!"

Oh my gosh, I'm thinking, were we crazy or what? But, I'm glad we did it, because sometimes, even if we don't know everything, maybe it is okay to take a leap of faith.

109

JUST LET IT RIP!

R obin (Bell) Dodson is a friend of mine. She is the sweetest person you'd ever want to meet. She is a devoted wife to her husband, Roy, a devoted mother and grandmother, and a former professional billiards player. Her claim to fame is that she won the WPA World Nine-ball Championship in 1990 and in 1991. She was also inducted into the Billiard Congress of America's hall of fame, and appeared on *The Tonight Show* starring Johnny Carson to demonstrate her incredible skills.

A few years back, Robin started a pool league at our church. We played in the summertime at different members' homes for two summers and I learned so much more about pool than I ever did playing in our basement with my two brothers. It was a blast, and addicting, especially if our team won. I do not know anything about how scores were kept. We just had good clean fellowship fun.

At the end of the summer, we had a pool tournament at a place in town called, Danny Kay's. Robin organized it all and it was a big deal! It was at this point-in-time, however, that fellowship gave way to a full-blown competition. But it was exciting!

We played *Nine-ball*, and if you ever saw Robin play, it was like "poetry in motion." Once she got her turn and first shot at the ball into the pocket, watch out! She just kept going and would get "all" the balls into the pockets as you stood by with your mouth open and watched. You were done! She won! Robin was fair and figured out the teams so it was more even, but Robin was not going to play down her highly competitive and award-winning skills for anyone.

Well, during one of our tournaments, it was my turn to come up against Robin. I mentally decided to push all anxiety out of my mind and thought, I'm just going let it *rip*! I'm just going to have fun! So, I did.

As I took up my cue stick and quietly concentrated on the ball it was like I was in my own world and felt so self-confident. My skills had also improved, and well, we played. I kept getting balls into the pockets and before I knew it, *I* had won! It was my one-and-only time beating Robin! I was so elated!

As I casually blew on the tip of my cue stick, I felt like a million bucks! Thanks Robin, for some good times! So, wherever you are in life, sometimes you just gotta "let it rip!"

110

SOMETIMES WE GET TO FEEL YOUNG AGAIN

When we were in junior high school and high school, we might have been asked to join the chess club, or ski club, or softball league or a bowling team. I played softball and was on an after-school bowling team. Those were the days.

In college, we maybe joined a sorority, a poetry club, or some sports team. I loved poetry so I took creative writing classes and became editor of our college magazine, *Sphere*. After college, in our great big move from Cleveland, Ohio, to New York City, my former husband and I, as young professionals, thought we were "so cool," being part of the "Preppy Movement," so I guess you could say we were part of the "Preppy Club." Some dear friends of ours had a Preppy party and a contest for the best dressed Preppy couple. We won.

As time moved on, we became members of the "Parents Club," when we exited to the suburbs. We got together with friends and family members for swim parties, barbecues, play dates, and holidays with our kids. Sometimes, we got to be "kid less," like the time we managed to enjoy a fancy dinner at a fancy restaurant in Manhattan. And, what did we talk about, over glasses of fine wine and plates of fillet mignon? Toilet training our toddlers, of course!

Before too long, we all joined the "40 Club," as our discussions turned to summer camps, baseball practice, gymnastics classes, piano recitals, ballet classes and other activities for our kids. Our lives revolved around an endless cycle of activities, but we did get together for parties, picnics, and some vacations.

All too soon, our kids were off to college and we joined the "Empty Nester Club." Like that TV series, *The Four Seasons*, some of us found each other again, and some of us moved on to find other people. We missed our kids, but were thrilled whenever they wanted to spend time with us. We kept working, or took up hobbies, or retired and traveled to fun places.

As time marched on again, we attended the weddings of our children, and later we joined "The Grandparents' Club." Being grandparents was great because we got to have all the fun cuddling with our grandchildren, playing with them, watching their first steps, and hearing their first words. We watched in wonder as we remembered our own children and mostly the joys of parenthood.

A little while ago, I joined "The Cataracts Club," and got new lenses. Are you there yet? If not, and you are like, thirty years old, your time will come, believe me! It was scary at first, before I realized how easy it could be. Fix my broken arm or broken finger, but *do not* touch my eyes! But I had an amazingly efficient and kind doctor, who made everything okay.

I guess there just might be advantages to growing older, as I am now amazed at how well I see! "That's better than I see right now!" exclaimed my younger daughter, Ashley. I am absolutely blown away at all the beautiful colors of flowers, and how green the trees are! And, the sky looks so blue! So, now you guessed it, I joined the "Off to See the World Club!"

111

THE HIGHS AND LOWS OF BEING A WRITER

Writing is not the easiest job in the world. It can be gut wrenching and energy draining, and make you feel like a failure sometimes because you must face rejections by editors or producers who can dismiss you in two seconds when you have poured your heart and soul into a body of work you are proud of. But rejection comes with the territory. "It's not personal," is a message I have heard my whole life. If one magazine editor did not want my ideas or articles, another one did. And sometimes you come close to making a deal with a studio and well, sometimes, someone did not like your ending on a screenplay, or, "here comes the writers' strike!"

The work can be discouraging and exhilarating because you put your heart on the line every time you write. You put your dreams on the line, and you work so hard, even in times of great stress, like raising kids or caring for a dying spouse. For me, writing is like breathing; the process is a joy. But, yes,

I have often dreamed of doing something else. For example, I always wanted to be a doctor or veterinarian and take care of elephants or people in Africa. But ever since I was sixteen years old, God gave me the gift of writing and that is what I do. My writing life has been filled with rewards, disappointments, and sometimes, embarrassing moments.

One time, I was getting assignments from the health editor of *The Dallas Morning News*. Not one to ever miss a call, I was getting my mail in my mailbox when I lived in Texas. I answered her call, and tried to sound professional as I realized I had stepped into a fire ant mound surrounding the mailbox post! I got the assignment, and bites from several fire ants.

Another time, I had the opportunity years ago, to write the honeymoon chapter for the book, *The Bride*, celebrating fifty years of *Bride's* magazine. It was a privilege and a joy to be part of this writing team, except when there were delays for whatever reason. I had to keep writing the honeymoon chapter as I went into labor with my first child. Fortunately, I got help from my mom after my daughter was born, so I could finish my chapter.

Still another time, I was writing a piece for *Hemispheres*, the *United Airlines* magazine, about Andrew Young, and his being the co-chairman of the 1996 Summer Olympics in Atlanta. Due to the time difference, me being on the West Coast, him being on the East Coast, I got up at something like four o'clock in the morning, plied myself with coffee, to interview him by telephone at six-thirty in the morning my time. We had a great interview, my article was published in *Hemispheres*, and circulated on all the *United Airlines* flights for a whole month. This was an article idea rejected by another prominent magazine, but accepted by the editor of *Hemispheres*.

Most of the time, writing articles has been a very rewarding experience, like the time I had the chance to take a transatlantic crossing on the *Queen Elizabeth 2* to interview Chef Bainbridge, and take a tour of the kitchen, featuring hundreds of pies! Or, like the time I had the opportunity to appear on the *Today Show* to talk about my first book, and sat next to the creator of Bugs Bunny, Friz Freleng, in the "Green Room." And, it was the experience of a lifetime to have coffee and a one-on-one, two-hour chat with Jeb Stuart, screenwriter of such fantastic movies as *Die Hard* and *The Fugitive*, at a writers' conference.

My writing has taken me on many journeys that I would not trade for the world, despite some heartbreaks and disappointments. I think I speak for many writers in that we always want to make a difference, think the best of situations, never give up hope, never quit. One article I wrote on tinnitus years ago for a magazine called, *Family Weekly*, was an interview with a prominent doctor who was working on a tinnitus masker to help people with this terrible condition. He was in Pennsylvania. When my article was published, he received hundreds of calls and letters from all over the world, including Egypt, thanking him.

This doctor thanked me, of course, and I felt so good in the knowledge that I indirectly helped others. So, if I have made you, my dear readers, laugh, cry, gain some knowledge or elements of reflections on life, then I am happy.

All those rejection slips I wall papered on my wall (metaphorically speaking), have been worth it.

A writer by the name of Bud Gardner once wrote: *When you speak, your words echo only across the room or down the hall. But when you write, your words echo down the ages.*

EPILOGUE
DO NOT LET YOUR DREAMS DIE

Everyone has dreams. Sometimes those dreams are realized with practically an army of supporters around you. Sometimes they are realized by accident, as God directs us to a different plan than what we thought we would be doing. And, sometimes, dreams come after many years of struggles. No dream is realized without a lot of hard work. But some dreams never get off the ground because of some cruel thing someone said or did to try to stop you. Do not let them! Press on, even if you must take baby steps every single day!

Several years after my first book was published were the worst years of my life. Imagine pouring your blood, sweat and tears into a book to help other married couples and parents, only to be asked by your father: "Did you have all your marbles when you wrote this?" My heart was crushed. And another person I loved tried to stop me from writing my book all together.

One evening, as I rose to give a speech at my hometown

bookstore, I could hardly speak. I felt like some imposter, despite receiving many compliments from my audience. For a while, I began to think my joy for writing was forever broken. And, to be honest, my father's words still sting a bit, but I have forgiven him, and others. I mustered my courage, determined to never stop writing. If you have dreams, but have been discouraged from pursuing them, I just want to tell you to never stop believing in your dreams, believing in yourself, no matter what people say. If it is an honorable dream and you want to help others, go for it!

In his amazing book, *Your Message Matters*, by Jonathan Milligan (*Baker Books*, 2020), he writes: *...the goal of life is to live our purpose, share our passion, and make a difference in people. Your best times are not behind you. They are ahead of you. Live this one and only life to the fullest...*

It does not matter your age. You are not too young, and you are not too old. It does not matter if some folks do not like your message or creation or invention because many others will. Time and your imagination are what you make of it.

God created you with certain talents and gifts and put a "dream" in your heart. He gives us strength to accomplish amazing things, and make the ordinary "extraordinary."

We see such actions of faith in a lowly farmer named Gideon in the *Bible*, who saved his nation. We see people down through the ages whose hearts were stirred with a desire to "make a difference."

I hope my stories have stirred emotions, desires, and dreams in your hearts. I pray that my words have helped you to appreciate the many small miracles in life, and the love of God, family, friends, and country. It is never too late to be the person God made you to be. And, as Milligan writes: *People are waiting for what you have to give.*

His Voice

By Anne Mount

One day God came like a whisper
and spoke to my heart,
I knew in an instant
that I needed to start.
He forever stands beside me,
to His love there is no end,
and so, I begin, again and again...

> *Go confidently in the direction of your dreams! Live the life you've imagined.* – Henry David Thoreau

> *Of all the roads she traveled, the journey back to herself was the most magnificent.* – SD

*Ten percent of all proceeds from each book sold will go towards Turning Point USA

ACKNOWLEDGMENTS

To my cousin, Louise Myers, for our many laughs we have shared together over the years; you are the sister I never had. May our continued lively talks and laughter always keep our dear moms in our hearts. To my cousin, Joe Accrocco, who always encouraged me with his words: "We're cheering you on!" Thank you.

Evonne Stokvis, dear friend, and Lindsay's mother-in-law, you are also like the sister I never had. May we enjoy many more incredible days being grandmas together with our adorable grandchildren. Thanks a million for your encouraging words that mean so much.

Sharrie Williams, you are a blessing and a treasure. Your encouragement, support and hospitality have been amazing over the years. Cheryl Ricker, thank you for your insights and prayers. To Publishing Director, Nick Poe, thank you for helping to make this book possible.

To Donna Cole, Gwen Oldfield, Jackie Bovi, Cookie Avila Currier, Shari Hawkins, Sally Cummins, Cindy Gunderson, Kyna Lumbreras, Linda Blay, Barb Creech, Cindy Schara, Cecelia Beverage, Yvonne Holdren, Grace Hockman, Melina Dani Piliero, Donna Jones, Judy and Al Rooks, Kathy Sasaki, Linda Balsamo, Lili Todora, Rob Marlett, Robin Arnold, Christine Currie, Sally Jaynes, Michael Arnold, Nadia

Zwayne, Nanciann Horvath, Pastor Bob and Becky Kopeny, and so many others, thank you for your friendship and prayers.

To my dear friends through the years, Rhea Zakich, Kathy Young Deegan, Roberta Hoechster, Joyce Ormsby Meyer, Nancy El Bouhali, Joy and Howland Blackiston, Marcia Lane Graeff, Georgianna Parisi, Nancy Emery Albert, Patricia Krul, Tina Stodd, Mary Brubaker, and Judy Rodgers, I'll always cherish the memories.

Special thanks to the readers of my many essays on my *Facebook* page (Anne_Mount), and of my former column, "Life As Is," that appeared in the "Lifestyles" section of the *Dayton Daily News*. Your expressions of delight and encouragement at my written words have kept me going during some tough trials. Special thanks to my Managing Editor, Mandy Gambrell. And to all my readers, thank you for going on this journey with me. May *The Other Side of Everything* elicit good memories of your own lives, offer encouragement for the difficult days, and conjure up bits of laughter, because laughter is not only good medicine, it is, as someone once said, a "mini vacation."

In the words of my friend and encourager from when I began writing and publishing my work at age sixteen:

When I stand before God at the end of my life, I would hope that I would not have a single bit of talent left, and could say: I used everything You gave me. —Erma Bombeck

We Are

By Anne Mount

We are the risks
We take,
The mistakes we make,
The prayers that shake
Our souls to care.

ABOUT THE AUTHOR

ANNE MOUNT is an award-winning poet, essayist, journalist, Literary Guild author, and screenwriter. Her work has been published in *Reader's Digest, McCall's, Redbook, Ladies' Home Journal, Bride's, Mademoiselle, Seventeen, Harper's Bazaar, Working Mother, Family Weekly, Lady's Circle, Hemispheres, American Baby, Childbirth Educator, Parents, Parenting, Child, San Francisco Chronicle, The Dallas Morning News, Marin Independent Journal, Dayton Daily News* and *The Cincinnati Enquirer*, among other publications.

She wrote a celebrity column for *Harper's Bazaar*, called, "Eye On," a consumer column for *Lady's Circle*, and most recently a column called, "Life As Is," for her hometown newspaper, *Dayton Daily News*.

She has been a senior associate editor at *Lady's Circle*, and an assistant features editor at *Harper's Bazaar*. In addition, she co-produced a radio show, *Sunday Night Live*, with Joanne Greene, introducing such authors as John Gray, Ph.D., *Men Are from Mars, Women Are from Venus*. At the time,

it was broadcast on the third largest radio station in the San Francisco Bay Area, *KFRC*.

Her book, *How to Stay Lovers While Raising Your Children*, (Mayer/*St. Martin's Press*), for married parents, was excerpted in three editions of *Reader's Digest* (USA, Great Britain, Canada), and reviewed in *USA Today*, *The Los Angeles Times* and numerous other publications. She appeared on the *Today Show*, and other television and radio programs. She is also co-author of the book, *The Bride*, (*Abram*), a celebration of fifty years of *Bride's*.

Mount has won numerous awards for her screenplays, including "Best Feature Screenplay," at the *Content 2020 Film Festival and Media Summit* for her screenplay, *Terror By Night*, a story about courageous faith.

She enjoys hiking, playing pickle ball, and spending time with family and friends.

www.ingramcontent.com/pod-product-compliance
Lightning Source LLC
Chambersburg PA
CBHW021500090426
42739CB00007B/405